Insider's Guide to Environmental Negotiation

Dale M. Gorczynski

Library of Congress Cataloging-in-Publication Data

Gorczynski, Dale M.
Insider's guide to environmental negotiation / by Dale M. Gorczynski
    p. cm.
    Includes bibliographical references and index.
    ISBN 0-87371-509-8
    1. Environmental policy—Decision making. 2. Decision-making,
Group. 3. Negotiation. 4. Pressure groups. I. Title.
HC79.E5G654   1991
363.7'0068'4—dc20   91-3893
                                                                       CIP

LEWIS PUBLISHERS, INC.
121 South Main Street, Chelsea, MI 48118

PRINTED IN THE UNITED STATES OF AMERICA
0 1 2 3 4 5 6 7 8 9

PREFACE

After eleven years on the Houston City Council, I discovered that I was an environmental negotiator. My good friend and fellow environmental conspirator Dr. Jack Matson suggested that I write a book that would serve as a practical guide to those who wanted to succeed at environmental negotiations. I was floored! What did I know about environmental negotiation? I asked Jack.

Jack Matson reminded me of my history. I chaired the City Council committee that got the raw sewage out of Lake Houston, a major source of drinking water for the City of Houston and an important recreational asset. I helped to persuade the Harris County Flood Control District and the Houston - Galveston Subsidence District that flooding and subsidence were directly related. I pointed out that in a flat area such as Houston (one foot of change in elevation per mile) even minor changes in the level of the land in relationship to sea level could have drastic effects on the area's drainage patterns. I chaired the Council committee charged with developing the Master Water Plan for the City of Houston. The plan found that to stop subsidence, the City had to stop taking so much drinking water from underground. The Plan called for the development of new surface water supplies from several places including the Wallisville estuary on the Trinity River.

The Wallisville Reservoir project was the ultimate environmental challenge. The water from the project would be badly needed by the City to supply its future drinking water needs; but building a fixed dam and sealing off the Wallisville estuary would cause irreparable damage to the fish, shrimp and oysters of the adjoining Galveston Bay. I have proposed a compromise.

Jack Matson told me that for the past eleven years I had worked on every type of environmental issue imaginable including the disposal of toxic wastes and the transportation of hazardous materials, the protection of park lands and the preservation of wetlands for migrating birds, the pollution of the water in our bayous and the high level of ozone in our air.

I had to admit that Houston had given me unlimited opportunities to perform good deeds on behalf of the environment, but was all of this work environmental negotiation and was I an environmental negotiator? After rolling these questions around in my brain for some time, I concluded that the very serious game I had been playing for the past eleven years was in fact environmental negotiation and that I was, can you believe it, an environmental negotiator.

I am willing to share with you the environmental negotiating secrets I have learned through eleven years of hard labor, but I do so reluctantly. It's not that I don't need the money that will come from this book. God knows I need the money. It's not that I don't know what I am talking about. If anybody knows how to play the game of environmental negotiation, I do. No, my reluctance in sharing these secrets comes from the fact that I don't know you and furthermore, I don't know how you will use the information contained in this book.

I do not know if you will use the new power this book gives you for good or evil. It worries me because the techniques, strategies and tactics I teach are effective and for the most part, morally neutral. You could use the lessons learned from this book to serve the environment or to destroy it. I worry about the uses that you will make of my work the same way a physicist worries whether his work will lead to abundant, cheap energy fusion or to a bomb that will end all life on Earth.

I give this book to you because I believe in people and I believe in you. You will see that you can play the game, you can win, and you can protect our world all at the same time. You will want to make wise environmental decisions because it is in your ultimate self-interest to do so.

As a final thought, relax. I know you are a good person, and you will do the right thing. If you are even tempted to use my secrets for evil purposes, just remember what the good reverends tell us: You will burn in Hell for knowingly doing evil.

(By the way, whenever I use the masculine "he" to refer to various players of the game, the feminine "she" is just as appropriate. The reverse is also true.)

FOREWORD

The old saying in negotiations is "You don't get what you deserve, you get what you negotiate." Dale Gorczynski's book reveals the negotiating process so that you can get what you deserve. Quality of life issues embodied in the word "environment" are significant, highly personal, and, as Dale points out, negotiable.

No one is better qualified to write this book than Dale Gorczynski. As a long-time member of the Houston City Council, he was present at the dawn of the awakening of the Houston environmental movement. He was a participant and a negotiator in all the significant environmental issues: air quality, subsidence and flooding, water and wastewater, environmental health, and hazardous wastes. Progress in these areas can be measured by his ability to resolve differences between parties. In 1984, he was given the Sierra Club's Environmental Leadership Award for his efforts in cleaning up Lake Houston.

An environmentalist by orientation, he has an equal ability to understand and interpret the diverse needs and interests of the business and industrial community, and he enjoys their respect. For several years in the late 1980's, he joined in an effort to bring new business to the city. Dale is a man of integrity, strong commitment, and high ideals.

As you read the book, Dale reveals his inner thoughts in a candid, overwhelmingly honest way. Having participated in many negotiations with him, I thought I knew it all. However, one insight immediately jumped out at me. I had never before realized that most of my negotiations had been indirect, through the media. Every time I went to the media, I was, in essence, commencing a negotiation. Now I have more sensitivity as to what I want and what my negotiating position should be.

Although the subject matter is environmental, it easily transcends the title and applies broadly to negotiations. His characterizations of players, the process, tactics, and potential outcomes have universal appeal. Now I deal with public officials with a newfound awareness of their psyches and limitations.

Lastly, Dale writes a book which will engage you with his easy conversational style, but which will sting you with fresh insights. This is Dale at his best, whispering in your ears his innermost secrets. The soul of this book is his soul. He has expressed himself in such a way that we all profit from the reading experience.

Jack V. Matson
Associate Professor of Civil and
Environmental Engineering
University of Houston

ACKNOWLEDGMENTS

Jack Matson was the catalyst who made this book happen. He made the suggestion that I write it, and he offered invaluable comments as the book took shape. Jack is an environmental engineer, a university professor, an author, an environmental co-conspirator of mine, and he is my good friend. I would never have begun this project without his encouragement, and I may never have completed it without his help.

I thank the staff of the University of St. Thomas library for their hospitality and for their patience. Special thanks go to Mark Landingham, St. Thomas reference librarian. I appreciate his amazing ability to locate any reference materials that I need. Mark provided more to me during the writing of this book than references, however. His enthusiasm, his wit, his insights, and his constant support enabled me to keep myself and this project on track.

Two University of St. Thomas faculty members gave me useful suggestions: Yhi Min Ho, economist and dean of the Cameron School of Business, and William Cunningham, career diplomat and head of the International Studies program. I thank them for their advice.

Chris Sagstetter, one of Houston's most successful environmental activists, provided tremendous assistance in preparing the hypothetical environmental negotiation you will find in the section on strategy. I wanted to create an imaginary example that would have a solid basis in reality. Chris helped me to do it.

I thank Cheryl Murray for performing all of the word processing that was required to produce the manuscript. I am grateful to her for her endurance and for her diligence. Gayle Gordon spent many nights editing the manuscript with laser-like precision. Barbara Link of the Citizen's Environmental Coalition offered several useful comments.

I tip my hat to the memory of Saul Alinsky, community organizing genius whose literary works gave me an understanding of the organizing process that I would never have had otherwise. I acknowledge the lessons I have learned through countless encounters with Alinsky's current-day disciples: Ed Chambers, Ernesto Cortes, Mike Clements, Sister Christine Stephens, Robert Rivera, and others. They have all had a powerful effect on my life and on my thinking about the political process.

Finally, I remember with love my father, John P. Gorczynski. One of the youngest children of a large Polish immigrant family, my father never attended college. In fact, he never graduated from high school. Yet he had a brilliant mind and an abiding curiosity about the ways of the world. He had an easy grace with words; and he used those words to make complex situations comprehensible, even to a young child. He taught me many things about life and about people, but most of all, he taught me what it means to care. I pray that this book is a fitting monument to his memory and to his name.

This book is dedicated to my wife,
Cynthia Canales Gorczynski,
and to our two children,
Christina and John
who will inherit the kind of world
we negotiate for them.

"If there is no struggle, there is no progress. Those who profess to favor freedom and yet deprecate agitation, are men who want crops without plowing up the ground, they want rain without thunder and lightning. They want the ocean without the awful roar of its many waters. This struggle may be a moral one, or it may be a physical one, and it may be both moral and physical, but it must be a struggle. Power conceded nothing without a demand. It never did and it never will."

Fredrick Douglas, 1857

TABLE OF CONTENTS

PART I:

INTRODUCTION

DEFINITION OF ENVIRONMENTAL NEGOTIATION

"Nature — pitiless in a pitiless universe — is certainly not concerned with the survival of Americans or, for that matter, of any of the two billion people now inhabiting the Earth. Hence, our destiny, with the aid of God, remains in our own hands."

Senator William Fulbright, 1954

Since the term *environmental negotiation* is a new one for both of us, let's spend a few minutes thinking about what it means. Let's try to define what it is we're talking about.

A short trip to *Webster's Third New International Dictionary* is a startling experience. The most common definition of *environment* is "surroundings." The number one definition of *negotiate* is "to communicate or confer with another so as to arrive at the settlement of some matter." If you combine the two definitions you get the following definition of environmental negotiation: "the action of communicating or conferring with another so as to arrive at the settlement of some matter related to the surroundings." If you say so, Mr. Webster, but it certainly doesn't sound like the kind of work I have been doing for the past 11 years.

We can do better. Reading further down, we find that Webster's definition of environment includes the following: "the whole complex of climatic, edaphic, and biotic factors that act upon an organism or an ecological community and ultimately determine its form and survival." Reading way down the list of definitions of negotiate we find "to successfully get over or across (as a road) or up or down (as a hill) or through (as an obstacle) as in carefully *negotiate* the winding road." Now we are getting somewhere. If we combine the two definitions and bias it a bit towards the human perspective we get:

> The process of successfully getting over or across or up or down or through the winding road of deciding the whole complex of climatic, edaphic, and biotic factors that act upon us and ultimately determine our form and survival.

I like this definition. It sounds a lot like the kind of work I have been doing for the past several years. It captures the sense of journey, the ups and downs and the curves and bumps in the road, that I experience when I am engaged in the process of environmental negotiation.

I feel that even this improved definition falls a little short in capturing the meaning of environmental negotiation because, to me, environmental negotiation is a game. Ouch! I can hear the howls of protest already. Environmental negotiation, a game? "Environmental negotiations are serious business," you tell me. "I am an environmental engineer," you say. "Environmental negotiations determine whether or not intelligent, scientifically correct solutions are applied to our pressing environmental problems." And I say to you, "Environmental engineer, you are correct."

Or you are a politician and you say to me:

> Environmental negotiations are serious business. My political survival depends on making the right choices during environmental negotiations. If I side too strongly with the environmental activists and the people of my district, I will lose the campaign contributions, the money that the developers and industrialists and other businesspeople send my way. If I side too much with the developers, industrialists, and other businesspeople, I could lose the votes and campaign workers that I get from the environmental activists and the people of my district.

And I say to you, "Politician, I understand. I've been there."

Or you are an industrialist or developer or some other kind of businessperson, and you say to me:

> Environmental negotiations are serious business. The outcomes of environmental negotiations determine whether or not I can make a living in my business. Environmental negotiations have profound effects on my profitability and on the price of my products, and on my competitiveness in the marketplace. We're not talking about a game, not when the survival of my business is at stake.

And I say to you, whether you are an industrialist or developer or some other kind of businessperson, "I understand, and I want you to succeed."

Or you are an environmental activist and you say to me:

> The decisions we make now during environmental negotiations will determine the future of life on this planet. The choices we make now will result in a future world that is healthy and beautiful and life-sustaining or in a world that is sickening and barren and deadly. Environmental negotiations are the human race's most serious business. These are not games we are playing.

And I say to you, "Environmental activist, I hear you, and I agree."

Then why do I call it a game if environmental negotiation is such a serious business? I call it a game for these reasons:

(1) To be a successful environmental negotiator, you need to understand that there are players, rules, strategies, and tactics involved in environmental negotiation, just as there are players, rules, strategies, and tactics when you play any other kind of game. The better you know your team's strengths and weaknesses, and the strengths and weaknesses of the opposing team, the more success you will have in environmental negotiation or in any other contest. The more you understand the rules of the game, and the wiser you are in tailoring your strategies and tactics to fit the rules and the players, the greater the probability of victory.

(2) The second reason I want you to think of environmental negotiation as a game is to help you to depersonalize, to detach, and to relax when you are involved in the process, i.e., when you are playing the game. You must learn to think of your opposition as the opposing team, not as the enemy, or worse yet, as the Devil.

The stakes are often high when you are negotiating critical environmental issues. Your opponent may seem ignorant or insensitive or uncaring. The opposing team may use deceitful and inflammatory tactics. Regardless of what your opponent does, you must not take it personally, and you must not lose control of your emotions or of the situation. If you use anger, make certain it is a cool, thoughtful anger. Diplomat Phil Jessup's advice is sound: "One maxim is never to lose your temper unless you intend to."

(3) Finally, environmental negotiation is an unusual game because if it is played very skillfully, both sides can sometimes win. If you view it as a war between the powers of the light and the forces of darkness, you will miss some of your opportunities for true greatness as an environmental negotiator. You must become flexible and creative, even playful, to imagine those extraordinary solutions that permit everyone to win. We have all seen athletic contests in which the performances were so impressive for both teams that we remarked, "It's a shame one side had to lose." In the game of environmental negotiation, there are usually clear winners and losers, but occasionally there are strategies, brilliantly conceived and carefully executed, that permit both sides to win.

In summary, I offer the following definition of environmental negotiation:

> Environmental negotiation is a game, a most serious game, that people use to decide the quality of their air, of their water, of their soil, and of the life around them. It is the cumulative outcome of these most important games that will determine the quality of human life and the future of all life in our world.

CHARACTERISTICS OF ENVIRONMENTAL NEGOTIATION

"Democracy is cumbersome, slow, and inefficient, but in due time, the voices of the people will be heard, and their latent wisdom will prevail."

Author Unknown
Attributed to Thomas Jefferson, but unverified

To be a successful environmental negotiator, you must understand the characteristics of environmental negotiations and how environmental negotiations differ from other types of negotiation. If you understand the unique nature of environmental negotiations, you will better understand the players, the styles, the strategies, and the tactics of the environmental negotiation game.

First, environmental negotiations are multi-disciplinary in nature. Environmental negotiations combine elements of science and engineering, politics and government, public health and public sensibilities, and economic theory and marketplace reality. It is the multi-disciplinary nature of environmental negotiations that make them especially difficult for those who would like to play the game. In order to succeed at environmental negotiations, you have to be prepared to work with many different kinds of people from many different fields of work and training. You have to be willing to learn the language and the issues, the rewards and the punishments, and the standards of success found in several fields outside of your own in order to be an environmental negotiator.

For example, if you are a civil engineer, you may understand perfectly how to clean up wastewater by building a sewer treatment plant. You know what type of concrete and steel to use. You know what size the plant needs to be to serve a given number of people and businesses. You know how to design and build the appropriate sewer treatment plant according to a budget and according to a timetable that you have established.

If you are an engineer, however, you probably do not know what the political consequences would be of locating your sewer treatment plant at certain locations in a residential neighborhood. There may be some locations in the neighborhood that the people would not object to as sites for your sewer plant. There may be other locations that would cause the community to come unglued.

If the people do rise up in arms to protest the site selected for your beautifully designed and technically correct wastewater treatment plant, what is it about the plant site that causes it to tread so heavily on neighborhood sensibilities? Are the people in the neighborhood concerned about how it will smell? Do they object to the idea of looking at it on a daily basis? Are they upset because a large park-like area of trees will be cut to build the plant? Are the people worried about the economic costs of the project? Will it make sewer rates go up, and will it make neighborhood property values go down?

If you are an engineer, you are going to need some help if you are going to get out of this mess. Fortunately, there are people who can help you. Politicians can suggest changes in the plant design or changes in the plant location that would make the project more acceptable to the local residents. Businesspeople in the community can explain how improving wastewater capacity creates greater opportunities for economic growth and for development. Realtors can evaluate the effect that the plant and its increased sewer capacity will have on property values. Public health experts can explain the improvements to public health and safety that result from more efficient wastewater treatment. Environmental activists can describe how better sewage treatment upstream greatly improves environmental quality downstream. The people in the neighborhood, and their leaders, will help you if you are willing and able to listen to them. Even the much maligned government bureaucrat can help you figure out how to pay for the project in a way that is as painless for the community as possible.

If you happen to be an engineer, please do not think I am picking on you alone. The same challenge of working simultaneously with multiple disciplines faces anyone who wants to be an environmental negotiator. Politicians understand politics and people's sensibilities, but they do not know anything about engineering or public health or ecology. Environmental activists understand ecology and public sensibilities, and some environmental engineering, but they frequently do not know about politics or how business works. The people in a given neighborhood know better than anyone how a project will affect their local community, but they often need the help of engineers, of politicians, of businesspeople, and of environmental activists in order to understand the larger issues outside of their local neighborhood.

Every successful environmental negotiator has the ability to work with people and with information outside of his field of specialization. Environmental negotiations favor the generalist, not the specialist. You must be willing to go outside of your discipline; there is no way around it. Multi-disciplinary experiences are essential characteristics of environmental negotiation.

Second, environmental negotiations may be done in public or in private, but there are always public consequences. People's health, safety, sensibilities, employment, income, and profits are affected by the outcomes of environmental negotiations. The public has the right to know what you and your opponent are deciding in your environmental negotiation.

You may not like the idea of the public sitting in judgement on the outcome of your negotiations. You may go to great lengths to keep the content of your decisions and the motivation for these decisions secret. "If I just handle this thing quietly, privately, the public won't find out about it," you think to yourself. You may even be able to persuade the opposing team's negotiator that it is in both of your interests to keep the matter a quiet, private little affair. You will argue that what the people don't know won't hurt them. The less said, the better. You will argue that the information is too difficult, too technical for them to handle; that it would only worry them needlessly if you told them about the risks they are facing. Besides, the risks are minimal, too small to count.

Your plan might work. You might succeed in keeping people outside of your negotiation from ever figuring out what your agreements were. The public may never know what decisions you made about their air, their water, their soil, their flowers, their trees, their birds, and their furry animals. The people may not even care.

But don't count on it. Because believe me, people do care. They care intensely about their environment. They care about it with a passion, with an emotional fervor, that starts with a small group of one or two individuals and spreads out to infect thousands and thousands. Huge, swaying masses of humanity care about the air they breathe, and the water they drink, and the ground they walk on. People care about flowers and frogs, about trees and clear, cold springs, about birds and furry animals with big eyes. People care about their health and the health of their children.

You may decide to try to keep the public from finding out what kind of decisions you are making, what kinds of plans you have for them and for their future, and you may get away with it. The people may never know, and they may not care.

But don't count on it. In trying to hide the results of environmental negotiation, you are trying to suppress some of the most primal urges in human nature. In truth, you are trying to hold down the power of humanity. People want to be healthy and they want their children to be healthy. They love beauty, particularly natural beauty, and they despise those who would destroy it. On the other hand, they care about their jobs and the amount of money they get to take home. They will respond violently to anyone who threatens their jobs or their take-home pay.

The public will want to know what your environmental negotiations have in store for them. You would be wise to remember that all of humanity is looking over your shoulder when you are engaged in your deliberations. The public has the right to know the results of your environmental negotiations, and believe me, the people will exercise that right sooner or later.

FORMAL AND INFORMAL NEGOTIATIONS

"He who knows the art of the direct and the indirect approach will be victorious. Such is the art of maneuvering."

Sun Tzu
The Art of War

There is a great deal more environmental negotiating taking place than most people realize. The term *negotiation* is seldom applied to environmental issues, however, because environmental negotiations do not fit the public concept of what real negotiations are supposed to look like. Mention the word *negotiation* and people think of diplomats sitting around a long table discussing arms control. Or they imagine a smoke-filled room where labor union representatives and company management staff wrestle for hours over wages, benefits, and working conditions. Or they see a group of businessmen working out a real estate deal as they enjoy lunch at an expensive restaurant.

All three of the above instances are examples of formal negotiations, the kind of negotiations that people usually think of when you mention the word. In formal negotiations, the parties involved have agreed to negotiate. They have acknowledged that the party or parties they are negotiating with are worthy opponents. There is the recognition in formal negotiations that all of the opposing sides have something of value to offer, that it is in everyone's interest to negotiate.

Formal negotiations must meet the following conditions:

1. All of the parties involved must agree to negotiate.
2. Each of the parties involved must believe that it has something of value to offer the opposing side, and that the opposing side has something of value to offer it.
3. There is mutual respect among all the parties involved; not necessarily affection, but certainly respect based upon the recognition that the opposing side has power and worth.
4. Each side believes it is in its own best interest to negotiate.
5. There is clarity on all sides regarding what issues are subject to negotiation.

These five conditions are rarely present during most environmental negotiations. Since most environmental negotiations are not formal ones, we fail to recognize them as negotiations at all. Environmental negotiations are taking place, but they do not look like negotiations because most of them are not formal.

Most environmental negotiations are informal negotiations. The five essential characteristics of informal negotiations are the complete opposite of the characteristics of formal negotiations:

1. All of the parties involved have not agreed to negotiate. In fact, in the case of informal negotiations, one or more of the parties involved are resisting any agreement to negotiate.
2. Several of the parties involved believe that they have nothing of value to offer the opposing side, and that the opposing side has nothing to offer them except grief.
3. In informal negotiations, there is the absence of mutual respect. Each side feels that it has the power and the moral license to do what it wants to do, regardless of the wishes of the opposing side.
4. In informal negotiations the opposing sides are not convinced that it is in their best interest to negotiate with each other.
5. There is no clarity in informal negotiations regarding what issues are to be acceptable topics for negotiations.

Let me give you an example that should highlight the differences between formal and informal negotiations. Suppose a company plans to build a hazardous-waste incinerator next door to your neighborhood. If you are a normal person living in an average neighborhood, your immediate reaction is one of anger and panic. "Not next door to my neighborhood!" you tell yourself. "Not next door to our neighborhood!" your neighbors agree.

Now, if you were living in a world of formal environmental negotiations, your neighborhood's initial anger and panic would be overcome by the desire to enter into reasonable negotiations with the company, and if this were a world of formal environmental negotiations, the company would promptly and genuinely agree to negotiate with the neighborhood. The company and the neighborhood would both see the value of negotiation in this situation. The two sides would show respect for each other. Both the people with the company and the people in the neighborhood would feel it was in their best interest to negotiate. Both sides would be clear regarding the central issue they were negotiating: whether or not to place a hazardous waste incinerator next door to the neighborhood.

In the real world as I have experienced it, formal negotiations are not what happens in this kind of situation. What normally takes place is a series of informal negotiations. Under these circumstances, the company often has no desire to negotiate with you and with the people in your neighborhood, particularly if the topic of negotiation is whether or not to build a hazardous-waste incinerator next door.

In addition, your neighborhood people are not especially anxious to negotiate with the company. They don't want to listen to the company's reasons for choosing their site. They don't want to listen period. They want the company to get the hell out of the neighborhood.

The company views you and your neighbors as being hysterical and self-serving. You and the neighborhood people see the company as being arrogant, insensitive, and uncaring.

Neither your neighborhood nor the company is convinced that negotiations are in their best interest. You and your neighborhood believe that any willingness to negotiate on the part of the company is a trick to persuade you to accept having a hazardous-waste incinerator located next door. The company believes that no amount of concessions or assurances can convince the neighborhood to accept the incinerator.

The company and the people in your neighborhood cannot even agree on the central question that is being negotiated. The company wants the question to be, "How long will it take before you neighborhood people accept the fact that a hazardous waste incinerator is going to be located next door?" The people in your neighborhood want the negotiating question to be, "How long will it take you, the company, to figure out that you can never build a hazardous-waste incinerator next door to our neighborhood?" Neither side is willing to negotiate the central question of whether or not a hazardous-waste incinerator should be located next to your residential neighborhood.

Informal negotiations, such as the one above, include a lot of negotiating foreplay. Neither partner is willing to "go all the way," and neither side is willing to make a commitment to a long-term relationship based upon mutual trust and shared benefit. Both the company and the neighborhood are interested in each other's behavior and in each other's reactions to certain stimulation, however.

Although informal negotiations contain a great deal of foreplay, foreplay can be very serious business. It would be a monumental mistake to presume that no important negotiating is taking place during informal negotiating foreplay. The fact is that both sides are exploring and are probing each other during foreplay. Each side is testing and stroking the other to see how far it can go.

The company wants to know how serious the neighborhood people are in their opposition to the incinerator. The company needs to learn what resources the neighborhood can bring to bear to stop the project. How many people can the neighborhood mobilize? How much money can they raise to fight the incinerator? Does the neighborhood have the ability to retain engineers, lawyers, and other hired guns? How much influence does the neighborhood have with elected officials?

The people in the neighborhood want to know how strongly the company is committed to the project. How much work and money has the company already invested in the project? Has the company purchased the land? Have they completed the engineering and design work? Does the company have the city, state, and federal permits required to build the facility? How much influence does the company have with elected officials? The company and the people in the neighborhood attempt to influence each other during informal negotiations, but both sides usually deny that they are negotiating.

Most environmental issues are resolved with only informal negotiations taking place. For example, your neighborhood could convince the company to go elsewhere to build their hazardous-waste incinerator, even though the company would never acknowledge that it was negotiating with you. Alternatively, your people may decide, after weeks or months of opposing the project, that the risk posed by the incinerator is acceptable and that it is not worth the trouble of opposing it. You and your neighbors may reach this conclusion without ever telling the company that locating the incinerator next to your neighborhood was a negotiable matter.

Sometimes informal negotiations evolve into formal ones. Be sure to notice if your environmental negotiations are changing from informal ones to formal ones because the unwritten rules of the game change dramatically. Informal negotiations are wild and crazy affairs. They are free-swinging, free-wheeling, and loud. The opposing sides routinely take shots at one another, often cheap shots. Insults, distortions of the facts, concealment of the facts, and ridicule are common practices during informal negotiations. It is common for both sides to make ridiculous claims and exaggerations regarding the positions of the opposing side. The differences are highlighted during informal negotiations.

Informal negotiations have the structure of an amoeba. There is very little accountability on either side. Each side can seldom be held responsible for what it says and what it does.

Formal negotiations are an entirely different matter. In formal negotiations, both sides have paid each other the supreme compliment of agreeing to negotiate with one another. There is an enormous amount of respect implied in that agreement. It is bad manners and, worse than that, it is bad strategy to act in formal negotiations the way you did during informal ones. It is counterproductive and foolish to ridicule your opponent and to persist in distorting his positions if he has shown you the courtesy and the respect of agreeing to negotiate with you.

It is wise to back away from the idea of emphasizing your

differences with your opponent if you both enter into formal negotiations. Consenting to formal negotiations does not mean that your opponent concurs with your opinions, and formal negotiations do not mean that your opponent has become your best friend. Formal negotiations do mean that your opponent has decided that it is in his best interest to try to resolve his differences with you through negotiations. If your opponent starts showing flexibility and movement on the issues, it may be appropriate to begin viewing him as your partner in problem-solving.

Accountability for words and deeds becomes a major factor in formal negotiations. You can make all sorts of wild statements about your opponent during informal negotiations, and, if they are not clearly defamatory, your opponent cannot hold you responsible for them. The reverse is also true. Your opponent can say all kinds of outrageous things about you and your position during informal negotiations, and you have little ground for complaint. In informal negotiation, neither side respects the other and neither side has agreed to negotiate. Almost anything goes.

During formal negotiations, you will be held accountable by your opponent for what you say and do, so choose your words and your actions very carefully. Under formal negotiating conditions, you have the right to expect your opponent to be acting in good faith. You have the right to hold him responsible for his words and his deeds. If you make a commitment to him during formal negotiations, he will expect you to keep it. If your opponent makes a commitment to you during formal negotiations, you have the right to expect him to keep it.

One of your first tasks as an environmental negotiator is to determine whether the issue you are negotiating is being handled as a formal negotiation or an informal negotiation. Once you have decided how your particular negotiation is being conducted, you will be able to select appropriate words, methods, and actions.

PUBLIC AND PRIVATE NEGOTIATIONS

"In statesmanship, get the formalities right, never mind about the moralities."

Mark Twain

There is a great deal of difference between negotiations that are carried out in full public view and negotiations that are conducted behind closed doors. The difference is not secrecy.

After more than a decade of involvement with all sorts of environmental negotiations, I am convinced that there is no such thing as secret negotiations. In my experience, a successfully kept secret in environmental negotiations is one that stays out of the newspapers for more than 24 hours.

People like to have secrets because it is fun. It is fun because you can share those secrets with all your friends. It is especially pleasurable to share a big secret with a friend in the news media. Of course, once you have shared your secrets with all of your friends, including those in the news business, your secrets are not secrets anymore. Everybody in town knows.

Always be careful what you say during environmental negotiations. Be careful what you say in public, and be careful what you

17

say in private. Be especially careful what you say to someone confidentially because, I promise you, it will not remain confidential very long. The difference between public and private negotiations is not secrecy.

The differences between public and private negotiations are the tone of voice you use and the volume of voice you use. When you are negotiating in public, you are constantly posturing for the benefit of the outside world. In public negotiations you use a loud voice and you use many grand gestures. Drama is an essential element of public negotiations. Private negotiations are far more subtle. The tone of voice is almost conversational. There is little jumping up and down for the benefit of the press and of the waiting public.

A useful way to contrast public and private negotiations is to compare the acting techniques used by stage actors and the acting techniques used by television actors. Stage actors are taught to play to the back row. They learn to speak loudly enough for everyone in the theater to hear them, even the person in the last row of the balcony. They use large, distinct, sweeping gestures so that even those sitting farthest away can see those gestures. Television acting is a much different enterprise. Television actors learn to play to the camera. The camera does not like loud noises or grand gestures. The camera likes normal conversational tones, and subtle, controlled movements.

It is the same with public and private negotiations. A public negotiation is like a large stage production. A private negotiation is like a TV talk show. You adjust your tone, your gestures, and your volume, to fit your environmental negotiation, whether it is a public one or a private one.

Be clear that the outside world will know the results of your negotiations, whether they are public or private. Be clear also that you are always performing during environmental negotiations. You are performing for your team's benefit, you are performing for the opposing team's benefit, and you are performing for the folks in the outside world who are following your negotiation. You are performing for all three groups, whether your negotiation is public or private. The difference is that you perform public negotiations in the style of a stage actor; you perform private negotiations in the manner of a TV talk-show celebrity.

Most environmental negotiations are public negotiations. Occasionally an environmental negotiation will combine public phases with private phases, but in these exceptional cases the public style of negotiating predominates. Private environmental negotiations are usually fleeting interludes between extended periods of public negotiations.

Now I should combine the informal and formal styles of environmental negotiations with the public and private ones. First, informal environmental negotiations can be either public or private, but they are most often public. In fact, informal public negotiations are the most common form of environmental negotiations. There are a handful of informal private negotiations. This type of negotiation is a somewhat softer, somewhat quieter version of the informal public negotiation. Second, formal environmental negotiations can be either public or private, but they are most often private. Formal private environmental negotiations are rare; formal public environmental negotiations are nonexistent.

As an environmental negotiator, you will be spending most of your time engaged in informal public negotiations. The skills and techniques of the stage actor are more suited to your work than the skills and techniques of the TV actor.

Because there are no such things as secret negotiations, remember that, regardless of the style you utilize, you are always performing to the world outside of the negotiations. The outside world is watching you. Be sure to give them a great performance.

HOW THE ROLES OF THE MEDIA CHANGE TO FIT THE VARIOUS KINDS OF ENVIRONMENTAL NEGOTIATIONS

> "The press is a sort of wild animal in our midst — restless, gigantic, always seeking new ways to use its strength."
>
> Zechariah Chafee, Jr., 1948

Let's spend a minute reviewing the previous material. Remember, there are formal and informal environmental negotiations, and there are public and private environmental negotiations. By far, the most common variety of environmental negotiation is the informal public negotiation. There are a few instances of informal private negotiations. There are only rare cases of formal environmental negotiations. Those few examples of formal negotiations always turn out to be private ones.

The media and the general public have a great curiosity about environmental negotiations. The media wants to know everything that is taking place everywhere. The media is genetically selected to be a compulsive busybody. The general public, the people, want to hear about things that affect them directly and personally. If the people believe that an environmental issue affects them personally, then their appetite for news about that issue is enormous. If the media and the public want to know what is occurring during environmental negotiations, they almost always find out. The media and the people find out what is taking place, and they usually find out very promptly.

Now let's examine the role of the media during environmental negotiations. The media exists to gather news and to report that news to the waiting public. The media always performs these two roles, the gathering of news information and the sharing of news, regardless of the variety of environmental negotiation game that is being played.

It is a major mistake to assume that gathering and sharing news are the only roles the media plays during environmental negotiations, however. The media performs several other critical roles. These roles vary to suit the kind of environmental negotiation game that is being played.

The influence of the media is always powerful, but it is most powerful during the most common environmental negotiation, the informal public negotiation. The media is such a powerful part of informal public negotiations that, without media involvement, no informal public negotiations would take place.

In addition to gathering and sharing the news, the media plays three critical roles during informal public negotiations. The three roles are as follows:

1.   Issue identification
2.   Issue definition
3.   Mediation

I will describe each of these three roles for you.

The first role of the media in informal public negotiations is *issue identification*. Until the media reports on an issue it isn't real. An old news reporter was asked, "What makes an issue newsworthy?" The old reporter replied, accurately, if not modestly, "My reporting on it makes it newsworthy." The media has the awesome power to create an environmental issue, just through the act of reporting on it. In reporting an issue the media give value and weight to it.

In the beginning stages, an environmental issue is usually the concern of a small number of people. Let us recall the example of the company that wants to put a hazardous-waste incinerator next to your neighborhood. In the beginning, you and the people in your neighborhood are deeply concerned about the issue. The company obviously has a strong interest in the matter. The rest of the world knows little about the issue, and consequently, could care less.

If the news media does a story on the proposed hazardous-waste incinerator, everything may change. An issue that only you, your neighbors, and the company cared about can immediately become a concern of the entire community. If you are lucky, once the media runs its stories, your issue may become an issue of importance to everyone.

It may be helpful to compare issue identification in environmental negotiations to name identification in politics. Issue identification is to environmental negotiations what name identification is to political elections. Both are a kind of valuable currency that can contribute greatly to your eventual success. Having people recognize your environmental issue doesn't guarantee your success in environmental negotiations any more than having people recognize your name guarantees that you will succeed in being elected to public office. It is difficult to imagine winning informal public negotiations without the people knowing your issue, however, just as it is difficult to conceive of someone being elected to public office without people knowing his name.

In addition to issue identification, the media also performs the role of *issue definition* during informal public negotiations. The media gives form and substance to the environmental debate. The media presents your arguments to the public, and the media also tells the people about the opposing side's position on the issue.

Although the media tries to be evenhanded and unbiased, it almost always slants the coverage of an issue in a way that benefits one side or the other. In the case of the incinerator, the media may make you and your neighbors look like intelligent, reasonable people courageously defending their homesteads. Or the media might make you out to be ignorant, hysterical people selfishly blocking a responsible proposal presented by private industry. The company might be portrayed by the media as being arrogant, insensitive, and heavy handed, or the media may present the company as being friendly, constructive, and patient.

The media not only causes the public to know about your issue; it also goes a long way towards defining your issue in the minds of people. Once the media has covered your issue, the people not only know about it, they have an opinion on it.

Finally, the media frequently acts as an active *mediator* during informal public negotiations. It ceases to be a mere observer of the proceedings. It is not uncommon for members of the media to act as go-betweens and as messengers for the two opposing sides.

You have, no doubt, heard a politician state at one time or another, "I never negotiate through the newspapers." The politician in this example is trying to convey the impression that he only negotiates directly with the opposing side, that he never uses the media as an intermediary. Any politician who makes this kind of claim should be viewed with considerable skepticism. I have never known a politician, or an environmental negotiator of any stature, who did not regularly negotiate through the newspapers, not to mention through the radio and through the TV set.

Every successful environmental negotiator makes heavy use of newspapers, of radios and of television to advance his or her negotiating position. A negotiator who doesn't use the media to advance his or her position is a fool. The politician who states, "I never negotiate through the newspapers," is really saying, "I do not like the way my negotiation through the newspapers is going."

The reporters covering environmental negotiations are often the only people talking directly with the two opposing sides. Remember, during informal public negotiations, each side refuses to negotiate with the other side. Many times during this kind of negotiation the two opposing sides will not even talk to one another. Both sides are usually willing to tell their sides of the story to the press, however. It is through the press that the two opposing sides discover each other's positions on the issue being debated.

It is through the press, it is with the press acting as mediators, that the two opposing sides conduct their informal environmental negotiations. Reporters shuttle back and forth between the two camps. The two sides give the reporters interviews. They shout at each other through the media, each making its case and each attacking the positions of the other side. The reporters fuel the negotiations by bringing each side the most recent views expressed by the opposing camp. The press is quick to highlight for each team any change of position or any movement by the other side.

Environmental negotiations conducted through the press are not necessarily elegant or beautiful to watch. Informal public negotiations often resemble the pre-event hype of a professional wrestling match. You have seen it on television. A nervous reporter gives each wrestler the opportunity to state his views regarding the upcoming match. The wrestler presents the relative merits of his position in comparison to those of his opponent. He outlines the type of outcome that he prefers, and he states the type of outcome that he anticipates.

In professional wrestling interviews, the interviewer does not confine himself to asking each wrestler questions. The interviewer always tells the interviewee what the opposing wrestler has said. This action on the part of the interviewer adds considerable heat, if not considerable light, to the overall conversation.

The same things happen in informal public negotiations. Reporters go to one side and say, "They said these things about you and your position. What do you think?" You, of course, tell the reporters exactly what you think, often in animated detail. Then the reporters go to the other side and they tell the opposing side what you said. Often the media performs this mediating role several times during a negotiation. As the media performs the role of mediator, a mysterious change begins to take place. The two sides begin to change their positions. Negotiations are taking place even though the two sides have not agreed to negotiate.

Not surprisingly, the media plays a much different role in formal private negotiations than it does in informal public negotiations. The media is a welcome participant in informal public negotiations; the media is usually an unwanted intruder in formal private negotiations.

In informal public negotiations the media links two unwilling parties together. It provides the means of communication between two opposing sides that do not want to talk directly to each other. The media provides issue identification and issue definition during informal public negotiations, and it acts as a mediator.

In formal private negotiations, the media is not needed to link two unwilling parties together. Formal private negotiations are, by definition, based on the fact that the two opposing sides are willing to negotiate. If two opposing sides are willing to negotiate face to face, there is no need for the press to act as a go-between. Formal private negotiations are based on the assumption that the two sides are able to state their respective points of view freely and directly. The media is not needed in formal private negotiations to identify the issues, to define the issues, or to act as a mediator. The two opposing sides perform all three of these roles during formal private negotiations.

In most private negotiations the two negotiating teams would prefer to be left alone by the media. It is much easier to hammer out agreements during private negotiations without the constant distractions and interruptions that are caused by the press. It would be nice if the media would just go away during private negotiations and allow the two sides to work out their differences.

The members of the media are, of course, not going to go away, not even for a moment. They have an enormous appetite for news and a huge desire to be part of the action. They interpret the word *private* to be a direct challenge to their constitutional rights to know and to say what they know. The members of the media seem to resent the diminished importance of their role during formal private negotiations as compared with their indispensable role during informal public negotiations.

The members of the press frequently respond to private negotiations by trying to destroy those negotiations. They try to goad the two negotiating teams into saying things in public that would have very destructive consequences for the ongoing, private negotiations. The media acts as an enabler during informal public negotiations. The media can become a full-blown *destroyer* during formal private negotiations if either side gives the media the opportunity to do so.

It is impossible to keep the media out of private negotiations altogether, but it is possible to limit the destructive role that the media often plays. Here are six simple rules for limiting the media's ability to ruin your formal private environmental negotiation.

1. Quickly reach a truce with your opponents regarding warfare through the media. Agree to cease and desist from attacking each other through the press.

2. Stop telling the members of media what your negotiating positions are. Persuade your opponents to stop giving their negotiating positions to the media.

3. Give generic, bland, vaguely optimistic statements to the press while you are conducting your formal private negotiation. Be positive, hopeful, and opaque when you are talking to the press during an ongoing private negotiation.

4. Once you reach an agreement with your opponents, offer to use a joint statement and a joint press conference to release your agreement. If your opponents are unwilling to have a joint press conference and do not want to issue a joint statement, decide with them who will announce your agreement to the press and when that announcement will be made.

5. If your opponents were genuinely co-operative during the formal private negotiations, let the media know it. Go out of your way to praise them for their constructive behavior.

6. If you are unhappy with the progress you are making through formal private negotiations, communicate that dissatisfaction directly to your opponents. It is rarely wise to complain to the press concerning your lack of progress with your private negotiation. If the formal private negotiation is not working for you, tell your opponents. If necessary, cease this type of negotiation with your opponents. Go back to informal public negotiations. Then you can say anything you want to about your opponents.

PART II:
THE PLAYERS
OF THE GAME

An Introduction to the Players of the Game

"You can't tell the players without a program."

John P. Gorczynski, my dad

When I was a boy, my father would take me to football games, to basketball games, and to baseball games in our hometown. He loved to watch athletic events, and I loved to watch them with him.

As we sat in the stands and saw the games unfold, my father would offer a running commentary on the actions that were taking place down on the playing field. He would compliment the players who demonstrated great skill or courage or foresight; and he would criticize those players who were incompetent or afraid or stupid.

My father gave his unsolicited editorials with fine precision. My father not only praised or condemned the players in a general sense, he called them by their names. It was not "The quarterback threw a great pass," it was "Steve McMillion threw a great pass." It was not "The centerfielder made a smart throw," it was "Huey Tarrant made a smart throw." My father could name every player on the hometown teams, and he could name every player on the opposing teams.

My father could call all of the players by name because he would always purchase a program before the start of each game. He was not comfortable seeing the game without having a program.

In one of our father-son rituals, I would usually ask him, "Dad, why do you spend money on a program? We can tell who wins without it, and it would be better to spend the money on candy." Each time I asked this question, my father would reply, "Son, you can't tell the players without a program." He gave this answer with seriousness and with conviction, as though profound meaning was contained in it.

It was not enough, my father seemed to be saying, to see the action and to know the results. To really understand, you had to have a program. You had to know the players of the game.

As I write this book, I am haunted by my father's words. I feel obliged to give you a program that will enable you to know the players of the environmental negotiations game.

In the upcoming chapters, I will tell you about engineers and politicians, industrialists and developers, lawyers and lobbyists. You will find out about the people, the bureaucrats, the environmental activists, and the media. I will even define for you some saintly types you have probably never heard of: translators, primary leaders, and bridgebuilders.

After reading this section, you will know the strengths and the weaknesses of the leading players of the environmental negotiation game. You will understand the roles they play in most environmental negotiations, and you will know how to use them in your specific environmental negotiations.

Take time to study "The Players of the Game" section. Remember, in environmental negotiations, just as in any other game, "you can't tell the players without a program."

ENGINEERS AND OTHER COOL, DISPASSIONATE, SCIENTIFIC TYPES

> "It is not enough that you should understand about applied science in order that your work may increase man's blessing. Concern for the man himself and his fate must always form the chief interest of all technical endeavors . . . Never forget this in the midst of your diagrams and equations."
>
> Albert Einstein, 1931

Engineers are a pain to deal with when you are attempting an environmental negotiation. They speak a language that 99% of the human race cannot understand. They have two hemispheres in their brains, just like the rest of us, but they insist on using only one of them, the logical, analytical side. Engineers, for the most part, don't know anything about politics or human nature. They affect an attitude of being above it all, above politics, above people, above everything and everybody.

Engineers and other cool, dispassionate, scientific types believe they are superior to the rest of us mere mortals because they have special knowledge that we don't have. They know how things work, and they know how to do things. They can change and shape the physical world to suit them. They understand the laws of the physical universe — why apples fall down and why a bridge stands up, why raw sewage is bad, nasty stuff and how to make that sewage nice and clean. Because engineers know how things work and because they can do things, we need them. They can help us figure out the answers to our more difficult environmental problems. That's why we put up with them. We need them to give us the right answers, the practical answers, the scientifically correct answers to our environmental troubles.

They can answer many of our basic questions. What do we do about dirty water and dirty air? How can we develop upstream and not cause flooding downstream? How can we build developments and transportation systems that serve our needs without destroying our natural world? How do we make products of convenience and of necessity without poisoning our land?

Whether we like it or not, we need these people. Engineers can be major players in the environmental negotiation game because they alone have the scientific and technical training necessary to solve our problems. They know the answers or, for a reasonable fee, they will find the answers for us.

We need them, but they are not easy to deal with. If you ask an engineer or some other cool, dispassionate, scientific type, "Do you think you are better than other people?" he might deny it. In his mind, however, he is saying,

> Of course I am better than other people. I went to school so that I could be better than other people. My education, experience, and training make me more knowledgeable, more rational, more objective than the rest of humanity. Others are driven by emotion, ignorance, and selfishness. I am an engineer. I am only concerned with the facts, the numbers, the cold, scientific truth.

Not surprisingly, people come to believe that engineers and other cool, dispassionate, scientific types look down on regular folks. This aloofness and air of superiority create a huge wall between engineers and the rest of the world. Their arrogance limits their ability to play the environmental negotiations game.

The language of engineers also limits their ability to shape environmental policies. If they cannot communicate with the world outside of their discipline, they have a severely limited capacity to influence that larger world. To get their message across, to have us understand the answers they are trying to give us, engineers have to be willing to speak our language, the language that regular folks speak.

Unfortunately, most engineers insist on speaking a language that makes no sense, even to the brightest among us. Their language is filled with jargon, with terms and concepts and abbreviations, that make them sound knowledgeable and impressive. But the jargon leaves the politicians, the businesspeople, the media, and the other major players of the game cracking jokes about the engineers and shaking their heads in confusion.

Because of their attitude of superiority and because of their inability or unwillingness to speak a language the rest of us can understand, engineers and other scientific types have trouble becoming major league environmental negotiators. Environmental negotiators usually use the engineers for two types of purposes:

1. They use engineers to mystify and to intimidate the less sophisticated players on the opposing team.
2. They use their engineers to duel with the engineers on the other team. This dueling-engineers contest is often a side-show to the real negotiating process.

After a brief time on stage, the engineers are often ushered off the stage and the real environmental negotiation continues.

I find these limited uses of engineers and of other scientific types to be wasteful and a little tragic. Engineers really do have a great deal to contribute to environmental negotiations. They can become major league players and big-time environmental negotiators in their own right, but only if they are willing to do the following:

1. They must drop their feelings of superiority and stop putting on airs. Engineers and other scientific types have to realize that, in the grand scheme of things, they are really no smarter, and no better, than the rest of us.
2. They must learn to speak a language that the rest of us understand.
3. They must be willing to learn about politics and about people and about how the environmental negotiation game is played.

If engineers and other cool, dispassionate, scientific types can achieve these three things, they can become powerful, successful environmental negotiators. We need to learn specialized knowledge that engineers and scientists possess. They need to learn humility, patience, and skill in communicating that knowledge to us.

POLITICIANS: ELECTED OFFICIALS AND THOSE WHO WANT TO BE

"And kid Congress and the Senate, don't scold 'em. They are just children thats never grown up. They don't like to be corrected in company. Don't send messages to 'em, send candy."

Will Rogers, 1932

"I always say, as you know, that if my fellow citizens want to go to Hell, I will help them. It's my job."

Oliver Wendell Holmes, 1920

"The hard thing is not to do what is right. The hard thing is to know what is right."

Lyndon Baines Johnson

Politicians are environmental players who carry around some big secrets. These secrets are never revealed to the world outside politics, and most politicians will not confess these secrets, even to each other. Many politicians will not admit to themselves that they have these secrets, even when it is quiet and when they are totally alone late at night.

The secrets I am talking about have nothing to do with sexual indiscretions or questionable financial transactions. The secrets I am talking about have to do with the methods politicians use to make decisions about the environment and other policy matters and the profound lack of knowledge that most politicians have while they are trying to make those decisions.

The Three Secrets of Every Politician

These are the three biggest secrets of every politician:

1. Ninety percent of the time, politicians do not know what they are talking about. Ten percent of the time, a politician's education, training and experience make him an expert on a given issue; the rest of the time the politician is flying the plane by the seat of his pants.
2. When politicians have important political decisions to make, they use the one-third, one-third, one-third rule. They give one-third weight to the *merits of the issue*; they give one-third weight to the effects a particular decision will have on *their voters*; and finally they give one-third weight to the effects a certain decision will have on their *campaign contributors*.
3. Politicians like to pretend that they know everything about every subject, and that they only make their decisions based on what is best for the people. They will lash out viciously at anyone who even hints at knowing or revealing their secrets. Let's talk about these secrets in more detail, and let's use elected officials as an example.

Secret Number One

Ninety percent of the time, elected officials do not know what they are talking about when they are confronted with an issue, environmental or otherwise. It doesn't matter if the elected official is a councilmember or mayor, state legislator or governor, member of Congress or the president. Ninety percent of the time when elected officials speak on an issue, they don't know what they are talking about.

Please do not misunderstand me. I am not saying that 90% of all elected officials are ignorant, uneducated people. Certainly some are brighter and better educated than others. For the most part, elected officials are about as ignorant or enlightened, as uneducated or educated, as the rest of humanity.

It is the nature of the job, not the qualities of elected officials, that causes them not to know what they are talking about 90% of the time. If you think about the tremendous variety of issues that elected officials face, it becomes obvious why they are in the dark so much of the time.

Simply stated, no matter what educational background or work experience you have prior to becoming an elected official, you will only spend about 10% of your time dealing with issues that your education and experience prepared you to handle. The rest of the time, you will be treading water in order not to drown. You will be attempting to reach the correct conclusions on subjects and issues about which you know little or nothing. In fact, my personal definition of an elected official is "someone who can speak at length and with great enthusiasm on subjects about which he knows little or nothing."

I know what you are thinking out there. "This secret would not apply to me," you are saying. You've been to school. You have your realtor's license, or you are an engineer, or you've run a business for 25 years. Perhaps you are an attorney, an expert in the field of constitutional law. You would know what you were doing more than 10% of the time if you became an elected official.

Fine, let's assume that you are a high-class attorney, an expert in constitutional law. You get elected to some public office, say, city council. When constitutional legal issues come up at city council, your face will beam. You will speak up confidently, explaining to all your colleagues the fine points of constitutional law. You will be comfortable in the knowledge that you really understand what you are saying, secure in the certainty that your colleagues on city council know almost nothing about constitutional law.

Your comfort will be short lived, however, because 5 minutes later the city council debate will turn to another topic, for example, solid-waste disposal regulations. You will attempt to maintain a confident, pleasant expression on your face, but inside you will be in a state of panic. What do you, a high-class attorney, know about solid-waste disposal regulations? "Nothing," you will whisper. You won't be able to recall anything in your education, training, or experience that has prepared you to speak knowledgeably on the subject of solid-waste disposal regulations.

If you are a city councilmember, however, you will not have the luxury of "sitting this one out." Decisions will have to be made regarding how your city is going to get rid of its solid waste. The TV cameras and the tape recorders will be rolling. The newspaper reporters will be taking notes. The lights in the room will be painfully bright, and the public will be staring at you. You will want to say, "Time out! I don't know anything about solid-waste disposal. I don't even know where to begin to learn about it. Let's go back and talk about constitutional law. I know that one cold."

But you cannot. You will have to listen closely to the discussion, read the written material you were given, use whatever common sense God gave you, and try your best to arrive at the correct decisions.

Five minutes later, you will be finished with solid-waste disposal; you will now be trying to decide whether or not to build a certain type of wastewater treatment plant. And guess what? You won't know anything about that subject either. As an elected official, you will experience the panic of not knowing a hundred times a day.

It is the nature of the job that makes elected officials ignorant 90% of the time, not the nature of elected officials. Elected officials have to make decisions affecting practically every aspect of human life. No human being is an expert in every aspect of human life. No human being is an expert in most aspects of human life. Most of us know quite a bit about a few things, and almost nothing about everything else. Elected officials and other politicians are like most of us.

To survive, elected officials rely heavily on their staffs; they become generalists, that is, people who are interested in learning about all sorts of things. They develop a keen sense of smell, a good nose for nonsense.

Elected officials learn to bluff and to bluff hard. They pretend to know what they are talking about all of the time, when at best they are comfortably knowledgeable 5 to 10% of the time. Elected officials are in the dark and they are afraid most of the time, but they hide their secret well.

Secret Number Two

Elected officials use the one-third, one-third, one-third rule in making major political decisions. They spend one-third of their time trying to figure out the merits of an issue. They spend one-third of their time trying to determine what effect a given position will have on their voters. They spend one-third of their time trying to decide what effect a particular position will have on their campaign contributors. One-third, merits of the issue; one-third, the voters; and one-third, the contributors. I will discuss each part of this three-part equation.

First, let's talk about the merits of the issue. Elected officials would have you believe that the merits of the issue test is the only test they use in deciding how to vote on an issue. "I only do what is best for the people of this city (county, state, nation)," they say. "I acted the way I did because it was the right thing to do," they proclaim.

President Lyndon Johnson was fond of saying, "The hard thing is not to do what is right. The hard thing is to know what is right." The clear implication of President Johnson's quote is that once he understood the merits of an issue, he had no trouble deciding what to do. His work was done. All he had to do was go out and do it. I do not believe it was as simple as that for President Johnson. I know it is not as simple as that for the elected officials that I have worked with for the past 11 years.

Elected officials are concerned about the merits of the issue. They are about one-third concerned. Before they decide what position to take, however, they also weigh the effects that a certain vote or a particular statement of position will have on their voters and their contributors.

The reason for their concern about the voters' reaction is obvious. No elected official can stay in office without the support of the majority of the voters. There is great truth in the old politician's saying, "There are politicians who cannot read, but there are no politicians who cannot count." Before elected officials take a stand on an issue, they try to weigh how many voters they will please, and how many voters they will offend, if they adopt a certain position. Obviously, elected officials are looking for stances that will cause their voters to cheer for them, not to throw rocks at them. If their position is not in keeping with that of their constituents, they become very nervous, and with good reason. If they go against the will of their constituency too many times, those elected officials will be looking for another job.

Besides the merits of the issue and the feelings of the voters, elected officials also have to pay attention to the desires of the campaign contributors, the money people. Some people are convinced that money, in the form of campaign contributions and in other forms, is the only thing most elected officials care about. I don't believe it. I've known too many elected officials at all levels of government — city, state, county, and federal — to believe that money is the only thing that elected officials care about. Money is not the only thing. It is not even the most important thing to most successful politicians. Money is, however, an important thing. It is about one-third important.

Money can be used to help elected officials, and it can be used to hurt elected officials. Campaign contributions can help elected officials stay in office, provided those contributions are given to them. Campaign contributions can also help defeat elected officials, if those campaign contributions are given to their opponents.

Money is a kind of political fuel. It pays for the campaign staff, the mail-outs, the yard signs, the radio and TV commercials, the phone banks, and the election-day card pushers. Money is not essential for success in electoral politics, but it is incredibly helpful. If candidates do not have money of their own, they have to persuade people who do have money to part with some of theirs. Even candidates who are wealthy do not want to spend their own money on a political campaign. They would much rather spend other people's money. So all elected officials and all candidates for public office try to take stands on the issues that are acceptable to the people who give money, the campaign contributors.

What if it is not possible to take a position that yields a favorable result for each component of our three-way test? What if it is not possible on a given issue to do the right thing, to make the voters happy, and to please the campaign contributors?

Under these circumstances, an elected official applies the one-third, one-third, one-third rule with an almost mathematical precision and predictability. If the merits and the voters are on one side, and the contributors are on the other side, the elected official will go with the merits and with the people. If the merits and the money are on one side, and the voters are on the other, the elected official will go with the merits and with the money. If the voters and the money people are in favor of a policy, and the merits of the issue argue against that policy, then the elected official says, "To hell with the merits of the issue." In the words of Scarlett O'Hara in *Gone With the Wind*, "I'll think about it tomorrow."

Secret Number Three

Elected officials will strike out at anyone who reveals the first two secrets. They believe that their continued success in politics depends on their ability to perpetuate the two myths that (1) they are completely knowledgeable about every issue that confronts them, and (2) they only consider the merits of the issue in deciding what position they will take on an issue. Elected officials respond with a rage that is frightening and dangerous if anyone starts to blow their cover by revealing the other two secrets I told you.

There is an important message in secret number three for those people who would like to win friends and to influence people who are elected officials. The message is simple: Never reveal secret one or secret two.

Be especially careful never to reveal that secret one and secret two apply to a specific elected official that you have to work with during an environmental negotiation. It is extremely tempting, but don't do it, not if you want the support of that elected official. The odds are overwhelming that the elected official with whom you are negotiating will not understand what you are talking about, particularly when the negotiations are just beginning. It is a certainty that the merits of the issue count for only one-third in that elected official's decision-making equation. But you are crazy to reveal these two secrets if you need, or want, that elected official's support.

BUREAUCRATS

> "Effective coordination requires disciplined performance, which cannot be achieved by supervision alone but must pervade the work process itself. This is the function of rules and regulations that govern operations whether they specify the dimensions of nuts and bolts or the criteria to be used in promoting subordinates. Even in the ideal case where every employee is a highly intelligent and skilled expert, there is a need for disciplined adherence to regulations."
>
> Peter M. Blau
> *Bureaucracy in Modern Society*

Bureaucrats, the countless people who run the governmental agencies of our country, suffer from too little pay, too much stress, and too little love. Sadly, they are held in universal contempt by the public they are supposed to serve. The public believes bureaucrats are inflexible, stupid, lazy, insensitive and uncaring. Without a doubt, many bureaucrats are all of these things. People often treat bureaucrats as though they expect the worst; bureaucrats frequently respond by giving it to them.

Because of the low regard and rough treatment they receive from the public, many bureaucrats suffer from chronically low self-esteem. The bureaucrats are not fools. They know they can receive better pay and better treatment almost anywhere in the private sector than they receive working for the government. Why do they do it? Why does anyone work as a government employee?

People choose to work for the government rather than the private sector for one or more of the following reasons:

1. They believe that working for the government offers them greater job security than working for the private sector. They are willing to take lower pay in order to receive greater job security.
2. They love public service; they believe in the work they are doing. They believe it is a good thing to serve their fellow human beings.
3. They believe they could not make it in the private sector. They believe there are problems with their resumes, with their personalities, with their backgrounds, or with their work habits that make them unacceptable to the private sector.
4. They view working for the government as an interim step towards a real job with real money in the private sector. They see government service as a rapidly turning revolving door. They will enter and they will stay in briefly, and then they will be propelled out into the good life in the private sector.

If you are engaged in environmental negotiation with a bureaucrat, you need to determine which of these reasons fits the bureaucrat with whom you are negotiating. You must tailor your approach to fit the reasons why your particular bureaucrat chose public service. If you do so, you will not believe how effective you can be in persuading your bureaucrat to move in your direction. Once you have determined which of these four reasons motivates your particular bureaucrat, you should always speak to those motivations when you are addressing that bureaucrat.

While there are many subtleties involved, I can give you four trustworthy rules that apply no matter what type of bureaucrat you are confronting. Here are four helpful hints for negotiating with any kind of bureaucrat.

Rule Number One

Never begin your negotiation by threatening to get him fired.

Although this approach seems a little overly aggressive and obnoxious to you, gentle reader, and you know you would never do this, you would be surprised how many times bureaucrats are threatened by the public with losing their jobs. "If you don't cooperate with me on solving this problem, I'm going to get you fired!" they are told.

This threat is a joke to the average bureaucrat. If he chose government service for the job security, he knows that cumbersome administrative procedures and civil service protections make it exceedingly difficult to fire him.

If he chose government work because he loves public service, he knows that he is a rose among thorns. The angry citizen who threatens to have him fired would only fare worse with the others in the agency.

If the bureaucrat took the government job because he didn't think he could make it in the private sector, the threat of losing his job seems absurd. "If this place would hire me," says the low self-image bureaucrat to himself, "then this place would hire anybody. I'm in no danger of losing a job at a place that is satisfied with anybody."

Finally, if the bureaucrat is looking at government service as a short ride through the revolving door on to the good life in the private sector, then it will be hard for him to keep from laughing out loud. "Before anyone fires me," he thinks, "I'm going to be out of here."

Rule Number Two

Never make a bureaucrat look or feel like a fool. I am not going to go through the list of four reasons why bureaucrats choose government work and explain to you why rule number two is a bad idea, regardless of which reason applies to the bureaucrat. You are an intelligent, competent individual. You can place this rule beside each of the four reasons previously stated, and you can easily determine why making a bureaucrat, any kind of bureaucrat, look and feel like a fool is not going to get you where you want to go.

And once again, I know you would never be so rude as to break rule number two. Your mama raised you better than that. You are a polite, friendly person.

Just in case you are tempted to lose your cool in the heat of the moment, however, let me compare bureaucrats to politicians. "Politicians," I said, "do not know what they are talking about 90% of the time." Bureaucrats work in a more limited field than politicians do; therefore, bureaucrats know what they are talking about much more often than politicians. But bureaucrats still do not know what they are talking about much of the time, and just like the politicians, bureaucrats resent bitterly anyone who makes that fact obvious. Bureaucrats are in need of being educated also — careful, subtle, sensitive education.

Rule Number Three

If at all possible, find the solution you want in your bureaucrat's book of rules and regulations. Every bureaucrat has a book of agency rules and regulations that he lives by. Bureaucrats are trained to go by that book. They are not rewarded for creativity, flexibility, or reasonableness; bureaucrats are rewarded for going by the book, never deviating. It is a rare bureaucrat, indeed, who will attempt to solve any problem in a manner that is different from the prescribed solution found in his book of rules and regulations. What if the book of rules and regulations is silent on the subject you need the bureaucrat to help you with? Then the bureaucrat will do nothing at all. Why? Because it's not in his book. Isn't the bureaucrat paid to think? No. The bureaucrat is paid to follow the book of rules and regulations.

The way out of endless debate with your friendly but unhelpful bureaucrat is to study the book of rules and regulations. Find the solution you want inside the book of rules, and gently suggest that solution to the bureaucrat. Because every bureaucrat is trained to apply rules and regulations, and because he is trained not to go outside of those rules and regulations, finding the solution you want in your bureaucrat's book of rules and regulations will give him great feelings of comfort and security. Bureaucrats trust the book of rules, they do not trust themselves. If you appeal to their sense of reason and their innate creativity as individuals, you will inevitably fail. If you show them that what you want is in their book of rules, then they will give you what you want, and they may even like you.

Rule Number Four

If the request you are making is a reasonable request, and the answer you are receiving from the bureaucrat is not a reasonable answer, then you are talking to the wrong person. Or to put it another way, if you are making sense, and the bureaucrat you are talking to is not making sense back to you, then you are talking to the wrong bureaucrat. There are many reasons why you could find yourself in this situation.

You might be talking to a new employee who doesn't know his job yet. There is a lot of turnover in many governmental agencies, and the new people always seem to be given the task of explaining the agency's policies to the public. You can improve your chances of success by seeking a more experienced person.

You could be talking to a bureaucrat in the wrong section of the agency, or you could be talking to the wrong agency entirely. If you are talking to a bureaucrat in the wrong section or in the wrong agency, you will never get what you want from him. Respectfully and humbly ask the bureaucrat in front of you for directions to the right section of his agency, or to the correct new agency. He probably knows the answer, and if you are nice, he will tell you.

You could be talking to a bureaucrat who is too far down the bureaucratic pecking order to make any independent interpretation of the rules. As I have said, bureaucrats are not rewarded for exercising independent judgement. They are rewarded for following the book of rules. Your question or your proposal may require a thoughtful interpretation of the rules. If this is the case, you need to move up the ranks of the bureaucracy until you find a bureaucrat with the authority and with the self-confidence to make an independent decision and to issue an opinion regarding your request.

Talking to the right level of the bureaucracy makes all the difference. I learned this valuable lesson while I was an undergraduate at Rice University. I was preparing a major term paper, and I found a particular book in the library to be especially important to my project. Because I knew that I would be relying heavily upon that book to complete my term paper, I asked the library desk clerk if I could check the book out for more time than the customary 2-week limit. The clerk said, "Absolutely not. The rule is 2 weeks check-out." I explained the importance of the book to my project. I tried reason, I tried charm, and I tried anger. The clerk would not yield. Two weeks was the limit. I asked for the head clerk, and I repeated the process, with the same result. Two weeks was the limit.

In utter frustration, I asked for the head librarian. The head librarian was not present, but the assistant librarian was. I explained to her my desire to check out the book for an extended period of time. I repeated the reasons why I needed the book for more than the customary time. The assistant librarian asked how long I wanted the book. I replied, "Four weeks would be fine." To my never-ending amazement, the assistant librarian said, "You can have the book for the 6 weeks remaining in the semester. If someone needs it before the semester is over, I will give you a call."

When I got to the right level of the bureaucracy, the absolutely binding rule of 2 weeks check-out magically disappeared. What works at university libraries also works at governmental agencies.

A Word About Department Heads and Directors of Governmental Agencies

Department heads and agency directors are more like politicians than they are like bureaucrats. The head of a department or agency got his job because of his political skills. He may have respectable professional credentials, he may be an intelligent person, and he may actually know something about his area of responsibility. But these things are not the primary reason why he got the impressive job title.

He got the big job because he favorably impressed the political figure or figures that had the power to appoint him. He got the job because the mayor, governor, or president wanted him to have the job. He is almost never protected by civil service, and he keeps his job only as long as his mayor, governor, or president wants him to keep his job.

Department heads and agency directors are far more interested in keeping politicians happy than the other members of the bureaucracy are. A low-level bureaucrat will religiously follow his book of rules and regulations. If the politician does not like the result, the lowest level bureaucrat will say, "Tough." The department head or agency director, on the other hand, does not care much about the book of rules and regulations. He cares about keeping the political official that appointed him happy.

If you find yourself negotiating with a department head or agency director, be sure to study the section of the book entitled "Politicians, Elected Officials and Those Who Want To Be". You may think that you are talking to a bureaucrat when you are negotiating with a department head or an agency director. In reality, you are talking directly to a skilled politician with a bureaucratic job title, and indirectly, you are talking to his political godfather who is peering over his shoulder.

INDUSTRIALISTS AND DEVELOPERS

"For years I thought what was good for our country was good for General Motors, and vice versa. The difference did not exist."

Charles E. Wilson Past
president of General Motors, 1953

"God gave me my money. I believe the power to make money is a gift from God . . . to be developed and used to the best of our ability for the good of mankind. Having been endowed with the gift I possess, I believe it is my duty to make money and to use the money for the good of my fellow man according to the dictates of my conscience."

John D. Rockefeller, 1905

Industrialists and developers believe they are the true heroes of this world. They take the raw stuff of nature and bend it to suit their will. Through their efforts, they create wealth and jobs and the countless benefits of modern civilization. Industrialists take thick, nasty crude oil and change it into gasoline, heating oil, plastics, and medicine. Developers take a swamp covered with overgrowth. They drain it dry, and erect luxury condominiums.

Industrialists and developers do not deny that they make money in the process. Although they are a little shy about admitting it, industrialists and developers are proud of the money they make. They believe they deserve every bit of it, and more. They are fulfilling human needs. They are making the world run. They are the doers, the builders. Every human being on Earth depends on them.

When industrialists and developers are producing their products, they are on a mission from God. They want nothing to stand in their way. To say they suffer from tunnel vision is to miss the point almost entirely. To industrialists and developers, the successful production of their products or the successful completion of their projects is not the most important thing. It is the *only* thing that matters.

What if an industrial process causes millions of tons of toxics to be released into the atmosphere? It has to be done. If the industrial process does not occur, then new wealth will not be created. Workers will lose their jobs, people will not have the benefits of the products produced, and the whole civilization will be set back.

What if draining a swamp kills hundreds of thousands of migratory birds? The project has to be built. If the project is not built, then new wealth will not be created. Workers will lose their jobs, people will not enjoy the benefits of the project, and the whole civilization will be diminished.

Industrialists and developers do not see themselves as evil destroyers of the natural world. They see themselves as heroes. Granted, a little self-serving, but heroes nevertheless. They believe they are doing what people want them to do.

Occasionally there are some environmentalists, or a few politicians, or a group of people in an adjoining neighborhood, who object to what they are trying to do. Industrialists and developers view those people who object as being a vocal minority.

Industrialists and developers believe that people who object to their actions are nuisances to be ignored or obstacles to be overcome. The objections raised by their detractors are of little concern to industrialists and to developers. What really matters to them is making the plastic or finishing the condominiums.

Government regulation is one of the most significant obstacles that industrialists and developers have to overcome. Elected officials are proud of their laws, and government bureaucrats reverently bow before their books of rules. Industrialists and developers have limited respect for laws and little patience with governmental rules and regulations.

Industrialists and developers often believe that elected officials and bureaucrats feed off the wealth that they, the industrialists and the developers, create. In their minds, they see elected officials and bureaucrats as needlessly complicating the real work of society.

The rule that industrialists and developers believe in most is the Golden Rule: "He who has the gold makes the rules." Industrialists and developers view elected officials and bureaucrats as being their personal hired hands. The government is there to serve them. When the government creates obstacles for them, when governmental regulation causes problems for them, then it is the government and its rules that must change. Industrialists and developers do not see themselves as creating any problems. To them, government is the problem.

Industrialists and developers believe that politicians and bureaucrats are infinitely pliable, provided a little money is expended in the right places and in the right ways. Campaign contributions; hunting trips; fishing trips; fancy dinners; tickets to the baseball games, the football games, the basketball games; bottles of wine and whiskey; and little gifts at Christmas time are all part of the cost of doing business. In the mind's eye of every industrialist and every developer stands a legion of groveling, obsequious politicians and bureaucrats with palms extended.

The influence of industrialists and developers on politicians and bureaucrats is considerable. For this reason, industrialists and developers should always be considered major-league environmental players. What they often lack in finesse, they more than make up for in raw power. Because they are such important players, industrialists and developers need to learn how to become constructive environmental negotiators; and every environmental negotiator needs to learn how to work with industrialists and developers.

Let me offer a little coaching advice for the industrialist or developer who wants to succeed at environmental negotiations. Your greatest strength is your single-mindedness of purpose. Your greatest strength can limit your effectiveness as an environmental negotiator, however. You need to realize that there are other people in the world who have goals that may be different from yours, and yet still compatible with yours. The people raising the objections may be willing to work with you. The environmentalist or the politician or the person in the neighborhood might be willing to sit down and work out a satisfactory compromise, provided you are willing to listen and to show respect.

My first suggestion for industrialists and developers is as follows:

> Listen to and show respect for those who object to what you are doing. Resolution of the conflict and successful compromise may be possible, but you will never know unless you open your ears.

My second suggestion for industrialists and developers flows from the first:

> Overcome the limitations of your tunnel vision by taking an expanded view of what is in your self-interest.

The toxic emissions your workers and neighbors breathe may come back to bite you in the form of higher health insurance costs and damage claims. The hundreds of thousands of migratory birds that rely on the wetlands near your condominium project may be a valuable tourist attraction, a natural asset with real economic values.

My third helpful hint for industrialists and developers would be

> Dare to be warm and compassionate towards people, and dare to care about the natural world.

Many industrialists and developers have totally unnerved their opposition by demonstrating real concern for people and a sincere commitment to protecting the environment.

The fourth and final thought for industrialists and developers to ponder is

> Understand that elected officials and bureaucrats exist to serve all the people. They are not your personal hired hands.

It is true that many of them are only too willing to serve your every need. Many of them are quite willing to be corrupted. Trust me, it is not in your long-term interest or theirs for you to succeed in corrupting them.

Now I have some suggestions for the environmental negotiator who would like to influence the behavior of industrialists and developers.

First, always state the changes you want by appealing to the self-interest of the industrialist or developer. Explain to him how it is in his best interest to have clean air to breathe or migratory birds flying overhead.

Second, be willing to praise him publicly. Industrialists and developers are used to being attacked by environmental negotiators. You will shock the hell out of him if you say something nice. You also make it even more in his self-interest to cooperate with you because he, like everyone else, wants favorable publicity.

Finally, tell the industrialist or developer that he is a hero and that you want him to succeed. Since he views you as an opponent and as an obstacle to overcome, he will be surprised, in fact, stunned, to hear that you appreciate the worth of what he is doing.

I have a warning, however. Flattery only works if you are sincere. If you see little or no redeeming value in what your industrialist or developer is attempting to do, don't lie to him. If he has done something worthwhile in the past, maybe you can point it out. He may have another product or project that you find worthwhile. You can raise these positive points as a way of letting your industrialist or developer know that you appreciate him, that you are on his side. You are especially on his side if he makes the necessary changes you want.

ENVIRONMENTAL ACTIVISTS

"The reasonable man adapts himself to the world: the unreasonable one persists in trying to adapt the world to himself. Therefore all progress depends on the unreasonable man."

George Bernard Shaw

Like industrialists and developers, environmental activists are people on a holy mission, a mission from God. Industrialists and developers are fanatic about getting things done. Environmental activists are fanatic about keeping things from getting done.

Environmental activists would rather be right than win. They seek perfection and purity, not compromise and victory. When, through their considerable efforts, they begin to reach their stated goals, they change those goals. They are forever moving their goal posts further and further away. They have an almost pathological fear of success, as though success would somehow taint them.

They view themselves as being separate from the world. The world is a dirty and corrupt place; environmental activists believe they are clean and incorruptible. To negotiate, to compromise, to achieve success in the world would be to become like the world, and the world is a bad place. They believe it is better to remain pure and separate from the world, better to strive for impossibly lofty goals than to compromise, to succeed, and to become part of the

59

world. Environmental activists believe it is better to be completely right and lose than to be mostly right and win.

Environmental activists are genetically selected to be independent, combative, and extreme. They do not agree with the masses of humanity, and they do not agree with each other. They have great difficulty taking a position on an issue because their position has to be a perfect position.

When environmental activists are gathered together to discuss an issue, they spend hours and hours discussing the issue in the most minute detail. Everyone in the room has an opinion, in fact, everyone in the room has several opinions. They argue back and forth with each other as though the fate of the world depended on their conclusions. Environmental activists do believe that the fate of the world depends on their decisions, so they take a great deal of time in reaching their conclusions.

One of the sad facts of life is that in a debate among environmental activists, decisions have to be unanimous for any action to be taken. If one person in the room refuses to agree to the correctness of a given position, then that position cannot be taken. Too often they define a correct position as being one that is so pure and so righteous that none of the faithful are opposed to it.

Their needs for unanimity and perfection make it exceedingly difficult for environmental activists to negotiate with anyone. Environmentalists are slow to take positions because of the need for unanimity and perfection. They are slow to change the positions they have taken because it is not easy to achieve unanimity and perfection all over again.

Because any environmental activist has a veto power over the policies and actions of the other environmental activists in his organization, a tyranny of the extremes reigns in most environmental organizations. The group cannot take a position or act on an issue until everyone, including the most extreme individuals, agrees.

Individuals with extreme positions are not, by nature, agreeable. All environmental activists are afraid of success, but those with extreme positions are most afraid of success. Extreme individuals are even afraid of success among other environmental activists. If the organization begins to agree with them, they will often move on to more extreme positions. Too many times, the organization will chase after them, begging them to consent to a position or to agree to a plan of action.

A lot of practicality, responsibility, and strategic thinking gets lost in the pursuit of pleasing the extremes. One crazy environmental activist can cause an entire environmental organization to take a stand that has no chance of success. Or that same crazy individual, by withholding his approval, can cause the entire organization to take no stand at all on an important issue.

If the individual environmental activist does not get his way, if the organization dares to take a position to do something without his permission, then that individual will frequently quit the organization and form a new one. There is the constant proliferation of new environmental organizations. Most of these new organizations have one chief and precious few Indians, but the members of the new organization are happy believing that they are pursuing the path of holiness and true perfection.

How can you negotiate with environmental activists? How can you negotiate with people who are seeking purity and perfection in an impure and imperfect world? How can you deal with people who do not believe in compromise and who are afraid of success? How can you work out reasonable and practical solutions with organizations that are frequently controlled by their most unreasonable and their most impractical members?

The answer is that you negotiate with environmental activists very selectively and very carefully.

First, select the environmental organizations and activists with whom you will negotiate. Do not attempt to negotiate with every environmental organization or every environmental activist. It is unnecessary and impractical to attempt to negotiate with the countless organizations and individuals who profess to have the right answer.

Second, negotiate with those environmental organizations or those environmental activists who are not afraid of success. Even a little reflection on this point during your negotiation will make it clear to you who is interested in successfully achieving a settlement, and who is more concerned with purity of essence and with posturing.

A third suggestion is to negotiate with leaders who have the courage, the credibility, and the stature to change their positions promptly if the circumstances warrant it. Do not negotiate with environmental activists whose feet are cast in concrete, people who are afraid to move even when movement makes sense.

My fourth piece of advice is critically important. Never give in to those who would require there to be unanimity in the environmental community in order for action to be taken. If they want to play that game within their own organizations, let them; but never impose the requirement for consensus among all environmentalists upon yourself. Cut your deal with the most credible and most reasonable organizations and individuals. Forget about trying to make everybody happy.

Finally, refuse to give in to the tyranny of the extremes. Once again, if the environmental organizations allow themselves to be controlled by their most extreme members, that is their choice. You should not spend your time and energy chasing after goals that are being moved further and further away from you.

My suggestions for negotiating with environmental activists are clearly useful lessons for the environmental activists themselves. If an environmental activist wants to be a successful environmental negotiator, he has to be willing to negotiate. The term *negotiate* implies movement, compromise, and less-than-perfect solutions. A negotiator has to have the confidence, courage, and power to modify his position in order to achieve a successful result. Organizations that do not permit their leaders to take positions or to change those positions in a timely fashion, destroy their leaders' ability to negotiate.

Environmental activists who want to be major environmental players have to persuade their organizations to eliminate the requirement of consensus. They must end the tyranny of the extremes. I am not saying it will be easy for environmental organizations to abandon these two long-standing traditions. I am saying that dumping these two unspoken rules is a necessity if environmental activists are going to be successful players of the game.

In spite of all the frustration you will experience in negotiating with them, it is necessary and it is worth it. Most environmental activists are sincere, intelligent, and deeply concerned about the future of the world. For all of their organizational and psychological limitations, environmental activists do shape the world. More often than not, there is wisdom, even vision, in the positions they so painfully arrive at. They often possess a goodness, a holiness, and a sense of commitment to their causes that gives them a power far beyond their numbers and far beyond their negotiating skills. Without a doubt, environmental activists are seriously flawed; and without a doubt, most of them are on the side of the angels.

THE PEOPLE

"I know no safer depository of the ultimate powers of the society but the people themselves; and if we think them not enlightened enough to exercise their control with wholesome discretion, the remedy is not to take it from them, but to inform their discretion by education. This is the true corrective of abuse of constitutional power."

Thomas Jefferson, 1820

"In this and like communities, public sentiment is everything. With public sentiment, nothing can fail; without it, nothing can succeed."

Abraham Lincoln, 1858

The people care deeply about environmental issues that affect them directly and personally, and they could care less about environmental issues that do not affect them in a direct and personal way. The location of a solid-waste landfill is an extremely important environmental issue to the people — to the people who live around the proposed landfill site. The rest of humanity doesn't give a damn where the landfill is located. Air quality is an important environmental concern for parents of children with asthma, the parents who have to take their children to hospital emergency rooms whenever the air quality deteriorates. Other people, for the most part, suck the air in and blow the air out without giving much thought to the volume of toxics in the air they are breathing.

People are seriously concerned about proper disposal of hazardous wastes if they live near a Superfund site or if they live close to a proposed toxic-waste disposal facility. They worry that their families, their friends, and they will die prematurely from cancer caused by toxic exposures. The people who live away from the real or proposed toxic waste site are mildly concerned at best.

It may be a sad comment on human nature to say that people only care about issues that affect them directly. It may seem profoundly cynical to say that they do not care about issues that do not affect them personally. It may be a sad statement on the human condition, but I assure you it is a true one.

"But I am not like that," you protest. "I care deeply about all of God's creation. I am concerned about the health and the safety of every human being on Earth. I worry about the survival of every living thing. I want to save the whales, the tropical rain forests, the Third World babies, the whooping cranes, the wetlands, the desert cacti. I am not a selfish, self-centered person. I care about every human being and every living thing."

My response to you is that you, in fact, may be one of today's living saints. You may be an environmental hero of the first order, willing to pledge your life, your fortune, and your sacred honor in the defense of the environment. Frankly, I doubt it.

I think it is more likely that you are like the rest of us. If an environmental issue affects you directly and personally, you are willing to give your time, your talent, and your treasure to the cause. If an environmental issue does not affect you personally, then you tend to be a great deal more philosophical about the matter. In theory, you may care very deeply about those issues that do not affect you directly. In reality, it would be hard for you to prove your concern by citing any acts of substance you have taken on behalf of those issues.

I am not saying that the people are not major environmental players. In any system of government that permits any reasonable degree of democracy, the people are the ultimate environmental negotiators. Though they are aroused slowly, and though they become involved very reluctantly, the people have an impressive way of resolving environmental issues and of achieving the results they want. The weight of public opinion is almost irresistible, provided it is properly organized and motivated.

Clearly, if the people care about your issue, if they support your position on the issue, and if they are willing to do something substantial about it, then your chances of winning on this environmental issue are enhanced considerably. If the people are aroused and they are with you, you have in your hands a powerful tool that can dramatically tip the outcome of the environmental negotiation in your favor.

I will discuss how you motivate people and how you influence public opinion throughout this book. Let me offer you a few reliable guidelines now.

First, explain to people why they should care about your particular environmental issue. People are busy, they have a lot on their minds. What is it about your issue that would cause them to stop, to listen, and to consider getting involved?

Second, tell the people how your environmental issue affects them directly and personally. Will they lose their jobs if a mindless regulation is imposed? Will they spend a fortune in medical bills if the ozone content is high in the air they breathe? Will their children die of cancer if they play on a toxic waste site? Will the ducks and geese they like to hunt disappear if the wetlands are destroyed?

Third, state why your specific position on an environmental issue is in their self-interest. Never ask the people for repeated, heroic self-sacrifice on behalf of an issue. Explain to them how adopting your particular position on the issue would improve their lives. Some examples would be a better economy, more disposable income, healthier children, better recreational opportunities, and so forth.

Finally, once you have the people's attention, and once they are committed to your point of view, tell them what specific actions they can take to bring about the results you both desire. For example, they could phone city councilmembers to complain about poor air quality. They could speak at a public hearing the State Water Commission is having on a permit to open a toxic waste site in their neighborhood. They could recruit new members to the cause by explaining the importance of the issue to everyone in the neighborhood. Once the people are on your side, you must always give them something useful to do with their newfound energy and enthusiasm.

Never expect the people to start out being as concerned as you are about your environmental issue. You probably did not start out being profoundly concerned about the issue yourself. It took you some time, you needed a thoughtful explanation, and someone had to persuade you to get involved with the issue. It will take the same things to convince the people to become involved with and supportive of your position.

Be patient. Remember, tell them why they should care about your issue. Explain to them how your issue affects them directly and personally. State the reasons why your position on the issue is in their self-interest. Once the people are with you, give them something useful to do.

If you cannot persuade the people by performing these tasks, then you do not deserve to win.

THE MEDIA

"To the press alone, chequered as it is with abuses, the world is indebted for all the triumphs which have been gained by reason and humanity over error and oppression."

James Madison, 1797

"Never get into a fight with a newspaper, unless you own a newspaper. And even if you own a newspaper, it's still probably not a good idea."

Homer Ford
Former Houston City Councilmember

"In America the President reigns for four years, and Journalism governs for ever and ever."

Oscar Wilde

A reporter holding a notebook, a tape recorder, or a TV camera is like a man with a loaded gun in his hands. He may use the weapon to help you. He may not use the weapon at all, or he may use the weapon to blow you away. Always remember the enormous constructive and destructive power that a reporter holds in his hands. Approach any reporter as thoughtfully, as cautiously, and as respectfully as you would approach any armed and potentially dangerous person.

Reporters shape public opinion, and public opinion shapes environmental negotiations. I am told that during the Russian Revolution Vladimir Lenin said of his political opponents, "Give them guns, but not the means of communication." He understood the extraordinary influence of the press. You will spend much of your time as an environmental negotiator utilizing the media to advance your specific cause. With the media's support, anything is possible.

Ironically, most reporters do not believe that they have real power. In fact, most reporters would claim that they are not players at all in the game of environmental negotiations. Their job, they would argue, is not to determine what environmental policies are adopted. Their job is merely to record and to present whatever policies the environmental negotiators agree upon.

Reporters, they would claim, are sideline observers; they are not part of the action. Reporters are not supposed to be part of the action. They are above the fray, objective, independent. Reporters, they say, do not seek to influence the current of human events. They simply observe, record, and report. They are dispassionate and ultimately disinterested regarding the results of environmental negotiations.

You, the environmental negotiator, would, of course, be crazy to swallow the myth of the powerless, objective, disinterested reporter. Reporters have extraordinary power. They use that power to further their personal careers and their personal agendas. Reporters are human beings with differing beliefs, values, and biases. During all the years I have been in public life, I have never met a reporter, whether he worked for a newspaper, a radio station, or a TV station, who did not have a preference concerning the outcomes of public debates. Every reporter has issues, opinions, and individuals that he favors. Every reporter has certain results that he prefers over other results. Those preferences, those biases have influence on his reporting.

I am not saying that every reporter is inaccurate or untruthful. Practically every reporter strives to be accurate and truthful. Most of the time, a reporter is accurate and truthful in what he reports. The real issue is not accuracy, the real issue is balance, fairness.

A reporter has a preferred outcome in mind. He consciously or unconsciously shapes public opinion by the manner in which he reports on an issue. Even more importantly, a reporter shapes public opinion by deciding what issues will be covered and what issues will not be covered.

I am sure that you are worried about the kind of news coverage you will receive as an environmental negotiator. Will it be positive or negative? Will the facts be correct or incorrect? How will you look and sound to the world out there? Will your issue, your point of view, be helped or be hindered by the news coverage you receive?

These are all legitimate concerns, but there is a larger question that should immediately pop into your head when you are thinking about the media. The first question you should ask yourself is, "Are they going to cover my issue at all? Are they going to tell my story?" It is all right to be concerned about looking good in a news report, but a more basic concern should be whether or not you will appear at all in the daily news.

The most common decision a reporter has to make is whether or not to cover a particular issue. The reporter asks himself a host of questions when considering whether to prepare a report on an issue. Is it newsworthy? Does it have media sex appeal? Does he know enough about the issue to do an intelligent story that will not embarrass him later? What other stories are available on a given day? How does this particular story compare with those stories?

The pressures involved with covering or not covering an issue are real. There is limited space in a newspaper and very limited time on television and radio. Reporters have rapidly approaching deadlines. In addition to limited time, reporters have limited energy. They have to choose what they will cover because there are more available issues on any day than all the reporters in the world could cover.

If you, the environmental negotiator, want to receive news coverage for yourself and for your issue, you are going to have to beat out almost all of the other potential stories that are out there on that day. Believe me, the fight to receive news coverage is fierce. Just about everybody wants to have his name in the newspaper and to see his face on the evening news. It is an adrenalin rush, an affirmation that you matter. Few people on Earth do not crave this natural high.

Now, you may be sitting out there thinking that you are different from the rest of humanity. You may believe that you do not want the coverage. Granted, there are times and circumstances in which no coverage at all would suit your purposes just fine. If you are attempting to do something that people would howl about if they found out, then you would probably prefer the lack of attention. Also, there are times when you want the media to report on your story, but not until you are ready. There are times when you want to hide out from the press for awhile until you are ready for your story to break.

If your environmental issue is important, however, you will probably receive some type of coverage, and you will usually want it. If your position on an issue is reasonable, thoughtful, and in the public interest, your environmental negotiation would almost certainly benefit from the exposure.

No coverage at all can be deadly for your negotiation, especially if your position is clearly in the public interest. If you have the right position on an issue and you can't get anybody to report on it, how are you going to shape public opinion in your favor? If you are right and nobody hears about it, then you are like the tree that falls in the isolation of the forest. Nobody cares because nobody hears.

Given that most of the time you want media coverage for your issue, how do you go about getting it? I believe that reporters use a mental checklist in determining whether or not to pursue a story. The checklist has five main items on it. If you can successfully address the five things on the reporter's checklist, you can greatly increase your chances of receiving prominent and favorable media coverage.

The Reporter's Checklist

(1) The reporter asks himself, "Is this story of sufficient weight to merit news coverage?" Does the story affect a large number of people? Or alternatively, does it affect a few people catastrophically? If the reporter does the story, the topic must be important enough for people to want to read about it or to hear about it.

(2) A reporter asks himself, "Does this story fit my medium?" If it is a story that has layers and layers of facts, then it is probably a

good newspaper story. If it is a story that can be described using three or four 15-second sound bites, then it is a good radio story. If it is a story that can be told quickly with a few chosen words and it is a story with a strong visual appeal, then it is a prime candidate for the most competitive medium of all, television.

(3) A reporter asks himself, "What will the superiors in my news organization think of a story on this subject?" Do they care about the issue? If they care, the story could get good placement in the newspaper or on the evening news. If they do not care, the story will not get good placement, and it may not run at all. Reporters regularly check with their superiors to make certain various topics are deemed worthy of coverage. Reporters listen closely to the signals they receive from their superiors. If their supervisors are interested in an issue, then the reporters are interested. If their supervisors are not interested in a particular topic, then the reporter's enthusiasm for that topic diminishes considerably.

(4) A reporter asks himself, "Do I know enough about this issue to do a decent story?" Does he have sufficient information on the subject? Has he asked enough people enough questions? Has he had time to verify the facts? Has he had time to process the information in his head? Reporters have strong legal and professional reasons for wanting to be accurate and thorough. The easier it is for a reporter to assemble and to verify the facts on an issue, the more likely it is that he will do a story on that issue.

(5) Finally, the reporter asks himself, "Do I care about this issue?" Some issues are compelling to an individual reporter, while other issues are of no interest to him at all. If a reporter is concerned about a particular issue, he is more likely to cover it. The opposite is also true. Since tastes vary widely among reporters, some are far more interested in environmental issues than are others. The reporters who are interested in environmental issues are the ones who will be doing stories about environmental negotiations.

To summarize, the reporter's five-part checklist for deciding whether or not to do a story is as follows:

1. Is the story of sufficient weight to merit coverage?
2. Does the story fit the reporter's medium?
3. Do the reporter's superiors in the news organization care about the story?

4. Does the reporter have sufficient information and enough time to process that information to be confident that the story is reasonably complete and accurate?
5. Does the reporter himself care about the story and the issue involved?

If you want news coverage for your environmental issue, you need to be aware of each one of these five questions. Knowing about each one of these five considerations does not guarantee that you will receive front-page placement in the newspaper, or that you will be the lead story on the evening television news. Not knowing about these five questions, however, will go a long way towards ensuring that you and your issue receive no coverage at all.

In addition to knowing the five questions that every reporter asks himself in deciding whether or not to do a story, there are some simple guidelines I can give you for improving your chances of receiving news coverage. Pay attention and follow these guidelines carefully. They work.

Guidelines for Improving Your Chances of Receiving News Coverage

First, be prepared to state clearly and concisely why your issue is important to the people in your news media's service area. Explain quickly and simply how your issue affects the people who buy the local newspaper or listen to the local radio stations or watch the local television stations.

Second, try to frame your issue so that it fits well with each of the three types of media — newspaper, radio, and television. Providing printed fact sheets and explaining how those facts can be verified will help you with every kind of media, but especially with newspapers. Speaking in clear, quick, catchy sound bites will help you with radio and television. It is important to capsulize your points early and often in your interviews. If at all possible, create strong visual images to go with your fact sheets and snappy interviews. Television reporters love to find visually exciting and descriptive images that they can use to tell your story.

Third, be willing to explain your views to the supervisors in the news organizations. Send the editors your packages of information. Offer to brief them on your issue. Do not think that you are wasting your time by talking to someone in the news organization who is not an easily recognizable reporter. Remember that those well-known reporters take their cues and receive their job performance grades from the lesser known but powerful editors and supervisors.

Fourth, give the members of the media the amount of information that they want, and give them as much lead time as possible to prepare their stories. For example, it always improves your chances of receiving coverage if you hold your press conference in the morning. Not the early morning, mind you. Reporters are not anxious to get up early in the morning to cover anything. Schedule your conference at 9:30 a.m., 10:00 a.m., or 10:30 a.m. By releasing your information in the morning, you are giving the reporters all day to prepare their story. You are giving them the time they need to process the information you have given them. They can verify the facts, conduct related interviews, write the story, and have it edited. By giving reporters a few extra hours to prepare their story, you make their lives a lot easier. If you make their lives easier, they will reward you by giving you more coverage.

Finally, make certain to involve those reporters who you know are personally interested in your story. Every news organization of any size has certain reporters who are clearly more interested in environmental issues. Be sure to include these reporters in all of your media activities. Do not assume that these environmentally minded reporters know what you are doing or what you are about to do. They may know your issue, but they cannot read your mind. Call them up and tell them what you are attempting to do. Explain to them why your issue matters. You cannot always select the reporters who will cover your issue, but you can always be sure to include reporters who are interested and sympathetic to your issue.

If you remember the five reporter's questions I gave you and if you follow the guidelines I have told you, odds are you are now receiving all kinds of news coverage. What should you do if, God forbid, they do a hostile story on you and your issue?

The first thing you should do is to relax. Don't panic, don't freak out. Take comfort in the words of Mae West, who reportedly said, "No publicity is bad publicity." There is real value to having your issue discussed, even if the reporting is not exactly to your liking.

Even if the reporter makes a serious error in reporting your story, never call him and scream at him. It is all right to point out errors and it is fine to ask that the errors be corrected, but you should always ask politely and respectfully. Remember what I told you. A reporter with a notebook, with a tape recorder, or with a TV camera is like a man with a loaded gun in his hands.

Never get into a fight with a news organization. They can hurt you a lot more than you can hurt them. You buy ink one pen at a time. They buy ink by the gallon. You are on TV and on the radio once in a while, if they decide to let you be there. They are on TV and on the radio every day. A deceased colleague of mine on the Houston City Council, Homer Ford, once told me, "Dale, never get into a fight with a newspaper, unless you own a newspaper." Then he smiled and added, "And even if you own a newspaper, it's still probably not a good idea."

The best strategy for coping with a bad story is usually to smile and to carry on. You need the media if you are going to shape public opinion. Holding grudges against reporters and getting into fights with their news organizations are expensive and foolish practices.

Lawyers, Lobbyists, and Other Hired Guns

"A lawyer has no business with the justices or injustices of the cause which he undertakes, unless his client asks his opinion, and then he is bound to give it honestly. The justice or injustice of the cause is to be decided by the judge."

Samuel Johnson

"It is not what a lawyer tells me I *may* do; but what humanity, reason, and justice tell me I ought to do."

Edmund Burke

"Everyone likes flattery; and when you come to Royalty you should lay it on with a trowel."

Benjamin Disraeli

In the days of the Old West it was common practice for two men to resolve their differences using the conflict resolution device known as the gunfight. The two gentlemen would agree that the town wasn't big enough for the both of them and that their differences were irreconcilable using other means. They would meet on the main street of town at high noon, face each other at an appropriate distance, reach for their guns, and settle the matter once and for all. Quick, direct, clean, and conclusive, the old-time gun fight had a lot to recommend it, unless you had slow hands and could not shoot straight.

If you did not have the skills, experience, or inclination to fight your own gunfights, there was a less courageous and more pragmatic alternative at your disposal. You could hire someone who was willing and able to do the shooting for you. You could retain the services of a hired gun.

Since we are all civilized now days, we don't use hired guns to resolve our differences. Instead, we get a lawyer, and for a fee, he goes and fights our battles for us.

I think it is useful to compare the motivations and behaviors of modern lawyers with those of the hired guns of the Old West. The similarities are a little startling. Let me list a few of them.

First, lawyers and hired guns place their talents and their loyalties in the hands of the person who has hired them. Secondly, lawyers and hired guns rarely have a personal interest in the issues being debated; lawyers and hired guns do what they do for business reasons, not for personal ones. Thirdly, lawyers and hired guns thrive on an abundance of conflict in society; the more hostility there is, the better it is for business. Fourth, lawyers and hired guns are both obsessed with their winning, and someone else losing. One failed negotiation would end a hired gun's career; several failed negotiations can end a lawyer's career.

Let me make it clear that I am talking about the motivations and behaviors of lawyers that I have observed repeatedly during environmental negotiations, not during courtroom proceedings. I have not seen lawyers in the courtroom. I do not know what lawyers do in the courtroom, or why they do it. I have seen the conduct of countless lawyers during numerous environmental negotiations, and I have a pretty good idea why they act the way they do.

During environmental negotiations, the lawyer's main offensive weapons are arrogance and aggressiveness. An engineer who is opposed to your position in a negotiation implies that you are a fool. An opposing lawyer states it outright. An industrialist on the opposing side will hit you about the head and shoulders with a blunt instrument. A lawyer will grab your throat, and he will squeeze down hard. A politician will cut you repeatedly, causing you to bleed from several small wounds all over your body. A lawyer will slash your arteries, hold them open, and bleed you dry.

The arrogance and aggressiveness of the opposing lawyer can be infuriating, particularly to the uninitiated. It is a normal human reaction to feel a sense of rage when someone is calling you a fool, squeezing down on your throat with both hands, and bleeding you white. It is easy to take the lawyer's assault on you personally.

It is important to your success as an environmental negotiator that you not take the lawyer's attacks on you personally. The lawyer attacks you in order to gain control of you. Your anger at him serves his purposes, not yours.

Few people can think and speak rationally when they are very angry. The lawyer knows that an outraged person is an easier adversary to manipulate than a cool, collected one. If the opposing lawyer makes you mad enough, you will start saying stupid things in retaliation. You will forget the strong points you wanted to make, and you will lose track of your carefully thought-out strategy.

Never let an opposing lawyer gain control of you by making you respond emotionally to his attacks and insults. Remember that it is not a personal matter to the opposing lawyer, it is strictly business. He has been hired to beat you. His goal is to win. He does not care about you as a person one way or the other. He is a hired gun; he could probably care less about the merits of the issues involved in your negotiations. If you remain calm and focused, you will be a far more effective negotiator. If it helps, think of him as the Old West outlaw wearing the black hat, and think of yourself as the fast-draw sheriff with the white hat. Smile serenely during the lawyer's withering fire, and you will drive him crazy.

The opposing lawyer will pretend that he has all the answers and that you have none. He is 100% right in what he is saying, and you are 100% wrong in what you are saying. He is a genius who knows everything, and you are a fool who knows nothing. Once again, don't let the opposing lawyer unnerve you.

His arrogance and his attitude of superiority are tactics he uses to weaken your self-confidence and your will to resist. If he can make you think he knows more than you do, he gains a useful advantage.

If a lawyer uses an attitude of arrogance and superiority, my advice to you is, once again, to relax and to smile serenely. In reality, most lawyers know almost nothing about environmental issues. Their strong suits are manipulating information and controlling human behavior. The odds are outstanding that you know far more about the issues involved than the opposing lawyer. If it helps you to remain confident, presume he is bluffing. He probably doesn't know what he is talking about, but you know that you do know what you are talking about.

If he catches you making a mistake, correct your error cheerfully and go on to build your case with additional, accurate facts. If you catch him making a mistake, and you certainly will, point it out in a friendly, instructional manner. You know environmental issues, he does not. You do not have to be obvious to make this point obvious.

In addition to being arrogant, lawyers are often stubborn and inflexible negotiators. They seem far more interested in winning than in resolving conflicts. They frequently interpret a willingness to compromise as a sign of weakness. Teams of lawyers who are opposing each other will want to continue to fight long after everyone else associated with the negotiations is prepared to settle. Lawyers often needlessly provoke conflicts, and they certainly needlessly prolong them.

I believe that lawyers tend to drag out environmental negotiations for economic reasons. Under most circumstances, lawyers bill their clients by the hour. The more billable hours a lawyer works, the more money he receives. It is not in the lawyer's economic interest to conclude an environmental negotiation in 10 billable hours when, with a little effort, he can make the negotiations require 100 billable hours.

Lawyers rival environmental activists in the practice of taking a position in negotiations and then not changing from that position. Lawyers and environmental activists both appear stubborn and inflexible during negotiations. The two groups' behavior, although similar in appearance, has strikingly different psychological motivations. The lawyer is inflexible because he wants to continue piling up billable hours. The lawyer is not particularly concerned whether or not the right thing gets done in the end. The environmental activist is intensely concerned that the right thing gets done, and the environmental activist is very inflexible about what is the right thing to do. Lawyers have limited personal involvements with environmental issues, environmental activists are consumed by their personal involvements with these issues.

In order for environmental negotiations to progress, it is essential to limit the roles of lawyers, just as it is necessary to clearly define the roles of environmental activists. View the lawyers on both sides of the negotiations as being taxicab drivers who want to keep the meters running. If the situation requires it, get all of the lawyers from all sides out of the room. Negotiate an agreement among the remaining parties, and then call the lawyers back into the room to put the agreement in writing.

Even your own lawyer will try to make you think you are incompetent to conclude a negotiation without him. He will tell you that you might do something unlawful without having him present to protect you. Take all of this hand-wringing by your lawyer with a grain of salt. You probably know the law well enough to avoid even the suggestion of something illegal during a negotiation. If you do propose or agree to something that has illegal elements, don't panic. The lawyers from both sides will quickly point out the illegality the second they are allowed back into the room.

Lobbyists

It is time to talk about a different kind of hired gun, the lobbyist. The motivations of lawyers and lobbyists are similar, but the behaviors of the two are strikingly different. I realize that many lawyers work as lobbyists. I am prepared to argue that lawyers who are working as lobbyists behave quite differently from lawyers who are engaged in other types of work.

Let me begin by defining a lobbyist. For the purpose of this discussion, a lobbyist is someone who is paid to influence governmental laws, regulations and actions. The term *lobbyist* comes from the time-honored lobbyist practice of waiting in the lobbies outside of legislative chambers in order to influence the legislators as they go to and from those legislative chambers. While the term *lobbyist* has its roots in legislative work, the changing shape of government has expanded the definition of a lobbyist. With the explosive growth of governmental regulatory agencies over the last several decades, with the expanded roles of county and of municipal government, and with the development of ever more sophisticated efforts to influence the executive branch of government at all levels, many people find regular work as lobbyists and never set foot inside a state or federal legislative hallway.

Lawyers and lobbyists are alike in terms of their motivations. Both lawyers and lobbyists give their talents and loyalties to the person or to the enterprise that has hired them. Neither lawyers nor lobbyists have strong personal interests in the relative merits of the issues that are being debated. Both make their decisions for business reasons, not for personal reasons. Both are obsessed with winning.

Lawyers and lobbyists behave differently, however. Lawyers begin their negotiations with arrogance and with aggressiveness; lobbyists start their negotiations with humility and with warmth. The lawyer from the opposing team will tell you that you are the enemy and that he is going to get you. A lobbyist from the opposing team will tell you that you are his friend and that he will help you get what you want. Lawyers overstate the differences between two opposing positions; lobbyists overstate the similarities. A skilled lobbyist would have you believe there is no difference between your position and that of his client. Opposing lawyers use personal attacks to control you; lobbyists use flattery and acts of "friendship." The lawyer will tell you how little you understand your issue; the lobbyist will tell you that you understand everything about your issue. The lobbyist will add that you have superior intelligence, come from a good gene pool, are physically very attractive, and are eloquent beyond description. The opposing lawyer will try to take your blood. The opposing lobbyist will try to take you to dinner or to the football game or to the opera.

The opposing lawyer will declare that he is your enemy; but at a personal level, he really doesn't mean it. The opposing lobbyist will declare that, at a personal level, you are his friend; but he doesn't mean it either. The lawyer's method is that of a mugger; the lobbyist's approach is that of a seducer.

Lobbyists are infinitely flexible in their efforts to seduce you. If you are the kind of person who is interested in making money and in finding loose women, the lobbyist will talk to you about ways of making money and places to find loose women. If you are interested in religion and in the Boy Scouts, then the lobbyist, the very same lobbyist, will cheerfully spend hours discussing with you the value of regular church attendance andin the sanctity of the Boy Scouts.

It is more difficult to resist a skilled lobbyist than it is to resist a skilled lawyer. The lobbyist acts like your best friend. He tells you wonderful things about yourself, things that you believe to be true. He says that there are only tiny little differences between your position and his position. With a few technical adjustments, your position and his position would be one.

If the seductive lobbyist starts making you weak in the knees, if you start believing that he is truly your friend, if you start believing that there is no difference between your position and his position, stop and remember this. A lobbyist is a hired gun. If you do exactly what he wants, he will treat you like you're his best friend. If you do not go along with him once or twice, he will act hurt and disappointed. If you cross a friendly lobbyist one too many times, he will grab you by the throat when you least expect it. And when he grabs your throat, he will squeeze down hard, just like a lawyer.

Translators, Primary Leaders, Bridgebuilders, and Other Candidates for Sainthood

"Some men see things as they are and say, why; I dream things that never were and say, why not."

Robert F. Kennedy, 1968

Our diverse, democratic, technologically advanced society could not function at all without translators, primary leaders, and bridgebuilders. All three possess special powers and skills that are of immense value to an environmental negotiator. These people are, in effect, modern-day saints who hold in their hands the keys to the Kingdom.

As an environmental negotiator, you must learn to recognize and to utilize them. They exist on your negotiating team, and they can be found on the opposing team as well. They are not always obvious or easy to identify, but they are always important.

Most of the people you meet in life are much less than they seem.

Translators, primary leaders, and bridgebuilders are much more than they seem to be. They are rarely arrogant or full of self-importance. A more common trait is an air of humility, a kind of New Testament meekness. Do not mistake their humility for lack of conviction or for weakness. In environmental negotiations, they are the people most likely to inherit the earth. I will define the terms *translator, primary leader,* and *bridgebuilder.* Then I will attempt to describe the characteristics of each of them for you.

A translator is a person with specialized training in science and technology who has the ability to translate the terms and the concepts of his field into the language and experiences of everyday life. Let me give you an example of a great translator.

Dr. Jack Matson is an environmental engineer and he is a friend of mine. Once he was called upon to explain the meaning of the term *leachate* to a group of regular folks. You know, leachate: "the fluid that has percolated through soil or other medium, a solution obtained by leaching." Leachate is an important term to understand if someone is planning to locate a sanitary landfill or a toxic-waste disposal site in your neighborhood.

Dr. Matson explained leachate in the following way:

> You know, when you set out a bag of garbage overnight, sometimes it rains on that bag of garbage. When you go to pick up that bag the next morning to put it out by the curb, a nasty, smelly liquid pours out of the holes in the bottom of the bag. That nasty, smelly stuff that pours out of your garbage bag, that's leachate.

Another outstanding translator is Dr. Paul Chu, University of Houston Materials Science professor and the world's leading figure in the field of superconductivity research. One magic afternoon, my 8-year-old son and I had lunch with Dr. Chu. My bright young son asked Dr. Chu to explain what superconductivity was and why it was so important. Dr. Chu did not give my son a definition out of a technical dictionary. Instead he told my son the following:

> John, if you ran down the hallway of your school, and you bumped against the walls all of the way down, you would be very hot and very tired at the end of your run. You wouldn't have much energy left to do anything else for a while. But if you ran straight down the hallway of your school, without bumping against the walls anywhere along the way, you would be cool and you would not be tired at the end of your run. You would have plenty of energy left to do other things.

Dr. Chu continued:

> That's the way it is with electricity as it runs along a pathway. Usually the electricity bumps against the walls so much that it is tired and has little energy left at the end. In the case of superconductivity, the electricity travels down the pathway without bumping into the walls and without losing energy. If the electricity travels the superconductive way, it has all of its energy left to do useful work.

After Dr. Chu's explanation, my 8-year-old son understood superconductivity and its importance, and so did I.

What is striking about both examples is the way in which both men made complex scientific concepts easily accessible to ordinary people. Both scientific experts used simple words and ordinary life experiences to explain difficult terms. In making science understandable, Dr. Matson and Dr. Chu made science real to the people listening. Those hearing the explanations were thrilled with the joy of understanding, and they were deeply impressed by the fact that these two brilliant men cared enough to communicate with them in ways that they could understand.

People have a profound appreciation for skilled translators. People are ready to follow good translators anywhere. That is why translators are so powerful in environmental negotiations.

The power of translators springs from two of our basic human desires. First, we want to understand what is going on in the world around us. Second, we want to be respected by those around us. Translators fulfill both of these basic human needs. Translators close the gap that exists between science and humanity. Translators believe that their science is important, but that human understanding is even more important.

If a scientist is willing to communicate with you in your language, he is telling you that you matter as a person, that you are worth educating and enlightening. If a scientist believes that you have worth as a human being, you are likely to agree with him on that point, and you are likely to agree with him on any other points he wishes to make.

Translators are out there. You may even be one yourself. Search for them, find them, and cherish them. Life is too short to be spent with people who increase your feelings of confusion and of worthlessness. Translators give you clarity, and they add to your self-respect.

Primary Leaders

A primary leader is, quite simply, someone who has a significant constituency who will follow him where he leads them. A primary leader is a person that others look up to; he is a guide to them in their decision-making. A primary leader has the respect and the trust of his following. When a primary leader tells his people that something is true, they believe him. When the primary leader tells them that it is time to act, they act; and they act in the way he tells them to act.

People follow a primary leader because he has the tools necessary to lead. He understands his constituency, and he is one with them. He can articulate their position on an issue intellectually and emotionally; he gives voice to their thoughts and to their feelings. He speaks to his people in a style they enjoy, but he can change his style when negotiating with those outside of his group. A primary leader has the intelligence, the empathy, the emotional stability, the eloquence, the integrity, and the strategic skills necessary to negotiate effectively on behalf of his followers. He is competent to lead them, and they know it. He is committed to their well-being, and they can feel it.

You can find primary leaders everywhere. They are in the local chambers of commerce, at the school PTAs, in the neighborhood civic clubs, in engineering societies, in labor unions, in churches, and in environmental organizations.

Primary leaders belong to one or more organizations, and they are usually the leaders of every single organization they belong to. A woman who is the president of the school PTA is also the chair of the church alter society. It turns out that this same person is also a youth sports coach at the YMCA and a den leader for the Cub Scouts. The man who is president of his engineering society is also the president of his neighborhood civic club. He also serves on the board of directors of the chamber of commerce, is a member of the parish council, and he, too, is a Cub Scouts den leader.

Leadership positions in multiple organizations are telltale signs of a primary leader. I am always struck by the fact that certain individuals find the time, the energy, and the commitment to be the leaders of several organizations, while the rest of humanity doesn't find the time, the energy, or the commitment to lead anything.

Another sure sign of a primary leader is the willingness to take a stand and to back up that stand with action. Most people have a hard time deciding what they believe and choosing what is important to them. Once they have decided what they believe and what is important to them, most people have even greater difficulty transforming those decisions into action.

Primary leaders are not paralyzed by indecision or inaction. They make up their minds what needs to be done, and then they go out and do it. More importantly, they bring others along with them. Their energy, their enthusiasm, and their commitment sweep many followers along. There is a constant bustle and activity surrounding primary leaders. There is an impatience with sitting still, with staying in one place. Life is only interesting to them if it contains movement, change, and challenges.

Not surprisingly, primary leaders are among the best environmental negotiators. They understand the issues and they know what is acceptable to their constituencies. They have the confidence to be flexible and to be creative, and they have the credibility and the power to sell an agreement to their people.

The ideal environmental negotiation is composed entirely of primary leaders. Ideally, only primary leaders should be allowed in the room during most of the environmental negotiation. If a person is not a primary leader, if he is not a legitimate representative of a significant constituency, then he often has no business being involved in serious negotiations.

I realize that there is a role for support staff such as engineers, lawyers, economists, and facilitators. But trust me, you will be far better off if you limit the role of all support personnel. The heart of the negotiation has to take place between or among primary leaders.

Try to have as many primary leaders as possible in support of your position, and be sure to involve the strongest and the sharpest ones in the actual negotiation. Identify the primary leaders of the people and of the organizations that embrace your point of view. Develop strategies that will make full use of their talents and of their insights.

If you can, only negotiate with primary leaders from the opposing side. Nobody else has the skills to strike a deal with you or the power to make that deal stick. The most frustrating experience in the world is to reach an agreement with the opposing side, and then to discover that the people with whom you've been negotiating don't have the standing to sell the agreement to the rest of their team. It doesn't matter how carefully you craft a settlement if the players on the other side of the negotiation do not have the power or the credibility to speak for their people.

When you engage in environmental negotiation, take your primary leaders along to do the negotiating. Negotiate only with the primary leaders from the other team. Do not waste your time with those who cannot deliver.

Bridgebuilders

Bridgebuilders are among the rarest creatures of God's creation. The natural state of human affairs is conflict. Environmental negotiations are no different. People divide up into opposing sides, assemble their troops, select their leaders, and go after each other. We admire and we fear those who are the most effective warriors on behalf of their position.

Bridgebuilders don't fit easily into our way of thinking. Bridgebuilders do not want to promote conflict, they want to resolve conflict. Bridgebuilders do not want to pick a side to fight for; they want to be on everybody's side. Like St. Francis of Assissi, bridgebuilders want to be instruments of peace and reconciliation. In environmental negotiations, bridgebuilders seek a conclusion that all the opposing sides can find acceptable.

Bridgebuilders have the credibility and the standing to be able to intercede in an environmental negotiation. Because they command the respect of both of the opposing sides, they can craft a settlement that is acceptable to all sides. Where are these modern-day followers of St. Francis of Assissi? The answer will probably surprise you.

Most of the environmental bridgebuilders I have known were politicians. I am not saying that most politicians are successful bridgebuilders, far from it. I am saying that, of the small handful of bridgebuilders that I know, almost all of them are politicians.

I have wondered why it is that certain individuals from the political ranks become almost saintly bridgebuilders. Politics is rarely considered a noble art. Politicians are not particularly high-minded, and they are seldom substantially better than the rest of humanity.

I think it is the psychological makeup of politicians that explains why most environmental bridgebuilders come from the political field. I have already told you several of the deepest secrets of politicians. It is time to let you in on another one.

Politicians want everybody to like them. Deep down, politicians want all the people to view them as being wonderful individuals doing terrific things. They are not satisfied with having some of the people like them, or even with having most of the people like them. Politicians want all of the people to like them.

It is, of course, impossible to get everybody to like you. It is a politician's dream, but it is a wholly unrealistic dream. Yet every politician I have ever known has been obsessed with trying to discover a way to make everybody happy.

Politicians handle this psychological need to make all the people like them in several ways. Some politicians attempt to tell each of the competing groups that make up their constituencies what they think each group wants to hear. These politicians hope that if they tell the various groups what each group wants to hear, their obvious contradictions will not be discovered and all the people will like them.

Other politicians divide up their constituencies into two main groups: (1) those whose opinions they care about and (2) those whose opinions they don't care about. These politicians try to keep the first group happy, and they try to forget the second group. The problem with this strategy is that it contradicts the primal desire of all politicians to want everyone to like them.

The need to make everyone happy paralyzes some politicians. They become so frightened at the prospect of someone not liking them that they refuse to do or to say anything. They hide out on the issues, they speak in ambiguous, muffled tones, and they take few actions.

A handful of politicians try to resolve their psychological need for everyone to like them by going into the business of bridgebuilding. These politicians are attempting to negotiate a risky and dangerous path.

Bridgebuilding is not for the fainthearted. Each of the opposing sides of a negotiation seeks to capture and to control the bridgebuilder. Each of the opposing sides may be suspicious of the bridgebuilder because he will not be captured or controlled by any side.

The bridgebuilder uses the respect and, perhaps, fear that he commands to make all sides negotiate in good faith. He prods the reluctant, he strengthens the meek, and he beats up on the bullies. He keeps his eye on the target. His goal is a reasonable settlement that is in the best interest of all parties. The bridgebuilder has the negotiating skills to create a settlement and the raw power to make that settlement stick.

Most environmental negotiations are conducted without the benefit of having a bridgebuilder involved. That is not surprising because most of life is conducted without having a bridgebuilder involved. If in your environmental negotiations you run into a bridgebuilder in operation, don't be startled. Remain calm. You are witnessing something rare and precious in this world. You are experiencing a human unifying force field. Cooperate enthusiastically with a genuine bridgebuilder. He will help you get what you deserve in your negotiations, and he will keep you from getting what you don't deserve. In both cases, the people's interests will be well served.

PART III:
STRATEGY

THE STORY OF SAM HOUSTON AND THE ALAMO

In the state of Texas, there are two holy shrines commemorating the two greatest battles of the Texas War of Independence. One is the Alamo, located in San Antonio, and the other is the San Jacinto Battleground, which is now on the outskirts of the modern city of Houston. The Alamo was the scene of heroic martyrdom and of defeat for the Texas Army. San Jacinto was the site of glorious triumph, the place where the Texas War of Independence was decisively won.

One man made important strategic decisions regarding both battles: Sam Houston. Careful study of the choices he made while serving as General of the Texas Army will help you appreciate the importance of strategy in your work as an environmental negotiator.

In his book *Lone Star, A History of Texas and the Texans*, T.H. Fehrenbach tells the following story. As Texas rose up in rebellion against Mexico, General Santa Anna, dictator and commander-in-chief of the Mexican Army, responded with a massive show of force. He brought approximately 6000 troops into Texas, determined to crush any pocket of resistance.

One hundred and eighty-two Texans, under the command of Colonel William Travis, decided to stand and to fight Santa Anna and his huge army at the Alamo fortress. As the oncoming Mexican Army began to encircle him, Colonel Travis sent out an impassioned plea for reinforcements to join him and his small group at the Alamo. In his letter, Travis vowed, "I shall never surrender or retreat." He continued, "If this call is neglected, I am determined to sustain myself as long as possible and die like a soldier who never forgets what is due his honor and that of his country. VICTORY OR DEATH."

Travis' cry for help reached the Texas Constitutional Convention at Washington-on-the-Brazos. There was an immediate call for the convention to dissolve and for the delegates to march to the Alamo.

Fehrenbach describes how Sam Houston reacted to this suggestion:

> Sam Houston, still on furlough from the Army, attended the convention as a delegate from Refugio. He was instrumental in beating down one wild notion that the convention adjourn and hasten, gun in hand, to the Alamo. Houston denounced this seemingly patriotic move as folly and treason to the people. He shouted that the Alamo was in its present straits because Texans had not made a government. He was heard."

A Texas government was promptly formed and Sam Houston was selected as general of the army. He started with four men under his command. While Sam Houston was assembling his army, the garrison at the Alamo was overrun by Santa Anna's army. There were few survivors.

Knowing that his small army was not prepared to confront the far larger Mexican Army, Sam Houston ordered his men to retreat eastward toward the United States. As his army retreated, it grew in size as new recruits from towns along the path joined the existing troops. Soon he had over 1000 men, a great improvement, but still no match for Santa Anna's forces.

Determined to catch Houston's army and to end the rebellion once and for all, Santa Anna divided his army into five parts. He took command of one group and he sent the four other groups in different directions with orders to find and to engage the Texas Army.

General Sam Houston continued to run from the approaching Mexicans. His soldiers were angry. They wanted to stand and to fight. The president of the newly formed Republic of Texas, David Burnet, protested to Houston, "The enemy are laughing you to scorn. You must fight them. You must retreat no farther. The country expects you to fight. The salvation of the country depends on you doing so." Houston ignored President Burnet, and he kept retreating.

Santa Anna's forces moved after Houston and his army. On the flat coastal plains between the San Jacinto River and Buffalo Bayou, Santa Anna was prepared to entrap the Texans.

General Sam Houston knew that his army was at its peak. Further retreat would cause many men to leave him out of frustration. Fehrenbach recalls:

> Houston deliberately let himself run out of territory, because he was running out of time . . . The evidence is that if he had turned away from the enemy at this time, the army would have revolted. The Texans were at the perfect pitch. They were tired, but not exhausted, angry, and murderous.

On the afternoon of April 21, 1836, Houston turned and attacked Santa Anna's army while the Mexicans were taking their customary afternoon siesta. Sam Houston and the Texans caught the larger Mexican forces completely by surprise. In a few short minutes, the Texans destroyed Santa Anna's startled unit of the Mexican Army. Santa Anna himself was captured. The Texas War of Independence was over. Sam Houston and the Texans had won.

The story of Sam Houston and the Alamo contains important lessons for environmental negotiators, as well as military strategists. Through his research, Sam Houston was aware of the size and the strength of the Mexican Army. He also knew how small and weak the Texas Army was. Taking stock of the situation, he knew it was hopeless for the Texans to engage the Mexican Army at the Alamo. He persuaded his government to get organized, and he himself organized the Texas Army. He continued his organizational efforts until his army was at its peak and until the opposing army was in a weakened condition. Then, when the time was right and when his troops were ready, Sam Houston acted, and he acted decisively. When Santa Anna and his troops chose not to take Sam Houston's army seriously, Sam Houston reacted with stunning effectiveness. He literally caught Santa Anna and the Mexican soldiers napping.

Sam Houston did his research, he took stock, he organized, he acted, and he reacted. These are the five strategic steps that make up the environmental negotiation process. As you study these five steps, think of General Sam Houston and the Alamo. Remember how well these five steps worked for the general.

AN INTRODUCTION TO STRATEGY

"I find the great thing in this world is not so much where we stand, as in what direction we are moving: To reach the port of heaven, we must sail sometimes with the wind and sometimes against it - but we must sail, and not drift, nor lie at anchor."

Oliver Wendell Holmes, 1891

If you have read this far in my book, you are now familiar with the special characteristics of environmental negotiation, you know the players of the environmental negotiation game, and you understand some of the rules that govern the various kinds of environmental negotiation. Now it is time for the real fun to begin. It is time to learn the strategy of the game.

Success in any game depends on a variety of factors: the skills of the players, the relative strengths of the two opposing teams, the strategies and tactics chosen by the team leaders, and, of course, dumb luck. I cannot help you with luck. If you are one of those people who was born lucky, don't apologize for it. Get down on your knees and thank God for it. If you were born unlucky, don't let your reoccurring bad luck cause you to give up. Lucky players can lose, and unlucky players can win in the game of environmental negotiation.

Although I cannot change your luck, I can improve your strategic thinking skills. I will act as an environmental negotiation coach for you and your team. If you listen to me and if you follow my advice, you will become a more successful player of the game.

Practice is, of course, necessary to improve any game performance. You learn by doing something, not just by reading about it. Your own creativity, enthusiasm, God-given talents, and personal stamina will determine how great an environmental player you ultimately become.

In addition to improving your strategic thinking, my coaching advice can also help to tip the balance of team strength in your favor. I want to be careful not to oversell my abilities in this regard. If there is a vast difference in the relative strengths of the two opposing teams, this book alone is not going to make all things equal. My advice will certainly strengthen your team and it will improve your chances for victory, but it is, at best, an incomplete remedy for the fundamental unfairness of life. If you have the attributes of David — courage, skill, creativity, strategic and tactical sense, and the will of God in your favor — then I can help you beat Goliath. If you do not possess the attributes of David, and if God is simply not on your side, then this book alone is not going to change the outcome.

In this section of the book, I will describe the five steps that make up the environmental negotiation process. The five steps are as follows:

1.   Do research
2.   Take stock
3.   Organize
4.   Act
5.   React

It is critically important that you understand these five steps and that you utilize each one of them in your strategic planning. Understanding these five steps and utilizing them correctly are the heart and soul of successful environmental negotiating strategy.

A successful strategy starts with reflection and planning. Organizing and decisive action follow.

Both contemplation and action are necessary for you to succeed. Environmental organizing and environmental action without contemplation and forethought are often baseless and ignorant. Environmental reflection and environmental planning without organizing and action are lifeless and wasted.

Serious thought is an essential part of each of these five steps, but I must emphasize that each of these five steps includes the essential element, action. These steps are all *active* in nature. They are active verbs. They are commands. As your coach, I am ordering you to perform all of these steps, and to do them with vigor.

STEP ONE: DO RESEARCH

WHAT KIND OF TRUCK IS ABOUT TO RUN OVER ME?

WHO IS DRIVING THE TRUCK THAT IS ABOUT TO RUN OVER ME?

> "Some problems are so complex that you have to be highly intelligent and well informed just to be undecided about them."
>
> Lawrence Peter, 1982

Most environmental problems and controversies are a case of one side attempting to drive a large truck over the interests and sensibilities of the other side. Environmental negotiations begin when one side believes that it has a problem with the current behavior, or the anticipated future behavior, of the opposing side. It is healthy human nature for us to be concerned about someone else's behavior when that behavior represents real or potential damage to those things in life that we care about. No healthy human being likes to be run over by a large truck, environmentally speaking or otherwise.

The shape and the size of the truck that threatens you depends a great deal on your point of view. As with beauty and other abstract concepts, environmental threats are very much in the mind of the beholder.

Let's imagine, hypothetically, that a company is planning to solidify toxic waste and inject it one-half mile underground into a salt dome near your neighborhood and local high school. The project, if constructed, will receive, store, process, and dispose of a wide variety of poisonous substances.

One branch of a bayou sits on the site and winds around close to the school. The site itself was historically used for agriculture, and there are numerous irrigation canals, reservoirs, and drainage ditches nearby. Children frequent some of these areas as local "swimming holes." In addition, the entire region is fairly flat, prone to flooding, and past floodwaters have caused damage to the school's pumps that furnish drinking water from two deep wells.

If your child attends this school, then you would view the proposed toxic-waste site as the environmental truck that is about to run over you. The other people in your neighborhood would almost certainly feel the same way.

But what if you are a member of the company's upper management? You would probably take a different view of the situation. Then, you might see the homeowners' objections as the environmental truck that is threatening to run over your corporate profitability. The neighborhood's opposition may seriously undermine your ability to conduct business at all.

During step one, doing research, you have to discover the shape and the size of the truck that is about to run over you. Specifically, what is it about your opponent's behavior that concerns you? What is he now doing or what is he planning to do that will damage the people and things that you hold dear?

If you are a homeowner who is fighting the proposed toxic-waste site near your neighborhood, you need to learn all about the proposed facility and its potential effects on you and your neighborhood. Exactly who is this company? Do they have a history of doing this sort of project? If they have built and operated toxic-waste sites elsewhere, were there any environmental problems associated with those projects? What is their corporate family tree? Is the company that is planning the toxic-waste site the parent company, or is it a subsidiary of a larger corporation?

You need to become familiar with the company's permit applications in order to understand what they propose to do in your neighborhood. For example, what kinds of toxic waste are going to be handled at this site? What are the chemical and physical properties of those waste products? Exactly how many shipments of toxic waste will go to the site? What products will be stored on the site and how much of those products will be stored there? How will they process the waste, and by what method will they dispose of it? What kinds of permits does the company need to obtain? What agencies will review the company's permit applications and who will issue the permits?

What effects would the proposed toxic-waste site have on you and the people in your neighborhood? Will there be releases, leaks, or discharges of toxic materials? Will the toxic materials get into the air? Will there be noxious odors? Will the toxic materials get into the water? What about the neighborhood children? Will the air be safe for them to breathe when they play outdoors? Will the children still be able to swim safely in their "swimming holes"? Will the fish in nearby waters be killed or contaminated? What will all of these possible effects do to neighborhood property values?

If you were a member of the toxic waste company's upper management team, you would attempt to learn everything you could about your opposition and its arguments. You would try to answer several questions. What is it about your proposed facility that the neighborhood objects to? Are there adjustments you could make in the location or in the design that would satisfy the neighborhood? What would be the cost of these changes and how would they affect corporate profitability?

Is the community's main objection to the facility the possible contamination of a large, nearby lake that supplies drinking water to a major metropolitan area? If this is the case, then you would want to learn a great deal about the current water-quality characteristics of the lake. Is the neighborhood's main concern the potential losses of their "swimming holes" and of their drinking-water wells? If these are the neighborhood's most important concerns, you would want to find out what effects your project would have on the "swimming holes" and on the wells. Are your opponents worried about the air quality in their area deteriorating? If deteriorating air quality in their area is their primary concern, you would want to study carefully what changes in air quality could occur as a result of your facility.

Most environmental negotiators do a good job of discovering the size and shape of the environmental truck that is about to run over them. Where they usually fall short, however, is in determining exactly who it is that is driving the oncoming truck. It is not enough to learn the size and shape of the truck.

If you want to stop an environmental truck from running over you, you have to know who it is that is driving the truck and what his characteristics are. What are his values and his habits? What are his temperament and educational background like? Who respects his opinions and whose opinions does he respect? What is his constituency? What is his economic influence? His political network? Why is your opponent trying to roll over you? What are his motivations? What are his possible alternatives?

Trucks do not steer themselves, and environmental crises do not often occur naturally. Environmental problems and confrontations are caused by and directed by certain specific prime movers.

It is critically important for you to be able to put names and faces on the people who are causing and directing your environmental problem. You have to learn who the primary leaders are, and you have to learn everything you can about them. You cannot prepare an intelligent strategy for beating the opposition without knowing exactly who the primary leaders of the opposition are.

If you are opposing a toxic-waste site, you have to know specifically who is driving the truck. It is not enough to know that the decision to build a facility near your neighborhood is supported by the company's upper management. Exactly who in the company's upper management is pushing the project? Who recommended it to the rest of the management? Who supervised the design of the plant? Who really runs the company? In other words, who in the company has the power to give company projects life or death? Through diligent research and intelligence gathering, you can learn the answers to these questions.

Company employees are an excellent source of information, but do not confine your investigation to those employees with white collars and with impressive titles. Almost any long-time employee of the company can give you the information you need. The company engineering staff or the management's clerical staff all have valuable insights to offer regarding who wields power in the company and how company decisions are really made.

If the company is a large, high-profile one, sympathetic reporters and politicians probably know how the company operates and who the key company players are. If you have good relations with your local media, with your local politicians, and with your local bureaucrats, you can get a great deal of useful, off-the-record information from them.

If the company is a small subsidiary of a larger parent company, you will want to know who calls the shots in the parent company. You will also want to know how much autonomy the parent company is giving its subsidiary.

Whether the company is large or small, there are some effective techniques for identifying the key decision makers. A Dunn & Bradstreet printout will identify the directors and officers of the company. It will tell you the financial condition of the company and identify its affiliated companies. It is always a good idea to talk to current company employees and current consultants for the company. Former employees and former consultants, if you can identify them, can provide a wealth of information regarding company decision-making practices. It is helpful to study any newspaper articles regarding the company and its leadership. You should not confine your newspaper research to the local papers. If the company or its parent company has sponsored similar projects in other places, get every available newspaper article from those places that discusses the company and its activities.

Use your own ingenuity. Think of creative ways to get the information you need. Do not break the law, do not engage in immoral conduct, and do not violate your sense of personal ethics, but get the information. Learn who the company's primary leaders are.

Let's assume that utilizing a variety of techniques, you now can put names and faces on the company's primary leaders. The company that is proposing to build the project is a subsidiary of a larger company. The parent company is not taking an active role in the project. The CEO of the parent company is basically a figurehead. He and the parent company lend credibility to the subsidiary.

The head of the subsidiary company is Ivan E. Thicke, company president and project manager. He is the most visible person associated with the project and he appears to be in charge. In reality, it is Erin K. Metall, chief engineering consultant for the project, who is the most important decision-maker. Erin K. Metall is the primary leader for the proposed toxic-waste project near your neighborhood.

You have also discovered the following about Ivan E. Thicke. He has an MBA degree from a prestigious university. He resides in Plantation Acres, an affluent neighborhood located many miles from the proposed site. He gives large contributions to school and community activities in the neighborhood of the proposed site. He has considerable influence with the local chamber of commerce. He is married, has one child, and portrays himself as being a family man and a good corporate citizen. It is important to him that the parent company views him as being an effective project manager.

Erin K. Metall, the chief consulting engineer and the true leader of the project, is an abrupt, somewhat arrogant professional engineer. He is the president of a major engineering firm, he has an international reputation, and he is considered highly competent by his engineering peers. He is proud of this reputation. Most of his social contacts are politically well-connected and usually wealthy. He is used to getting his way. He sees himself as being a tough, no-nonsense, professional engineer. He has little concern about public relations. He does not care what the public thinks about him and his projects. His main interest is in pleasing the corporate, deep-pocket individuals that fund his projects.

Ivan E. Thicke is very concerned about opposition to the project and about how that opposition could affect corporate-community relations. He would prefer to win over the opposition rather than defeat it.

Erin K. Metall wants the project to begin immediately. He views the neighborhood opposition as being ignorant, obstinate, and misguided.

Clearly, by assembling all of the information above, you were able to put names and faces on the primary leaders behind the proposed toxic-waste facility. You now know the most important people who are driving the environmental truck that is about to run over you. You know that if your strategy is going to be successful, you have to figure out a way to deal with Ivan E. Thicke and Erin K. Metall.

If you are a member of the company's management team, you must go through the same process of putting names and faces on the primary leaders of the opposing team. Through research and legitimate intelligence gathering, you have discovered who is leading the charge against you and your company.

By examining local newspaper articles and by talking to community people, you have discovered that Connie Kubiak, a mother of two children in the neighborhood school, is the individual driving the truck for the community. She is a past president and a past program chair for the school PTA. At one time or another, she has held all of the major offices in her civic club: president, secretary, and treasurer. Connie chaired the committee that succeeded in establishing the first community center in her neighborhood. Clearly, Connie Kubiak is a primary leader in her neighborhood of Hudson Hollow. She has a major constituency, and she can deliver that constituency for the causes she supports.

She has a variety of concerns about the proposed toxic-waste project. She is worried about potential contamination of area water wells, especially those that serve the schools. She knows that the proposed site has experienced flooding in the past and that it will certainly experience flooding in the future. Wastes that are transported to the site, or that are stored on the site, could leak during flooding and be carried throughout the area. If this were to happen, the children's "swimming holes" would be unsafe due to the presence of toxic wastes. She knows that the Air Control Board has identified 37 possible health effects that could result from toxic air emissions caused by the facility.

She has also discovered that there are several fault lines in the area and that there is evidence of extensive oil-field drilling in the salt dome area where the toxic waste is to be stored. These fault lines and drilling holes could be avenues of migration that could take the toxic waste into the underground aquifers.

Although the people in her area do not drink the water from Lake Blackburn, Connie Kubiak is also concerned that toxic wastes from the site could find their way into the lake during heavy rains and flooding. She knows Lake Blackburn is the major source of drinking water for the large metropolitan area a few miles from her neighborhood.

Whether you are from the neighborhood or from the company's management, you have to complete the research step before you can design a winning strategy for your environmental negotiation. After completing step one, you know the size and shape of the environmental problem confronting you, and you know the primary leaders of the team opposing you. You are well on your way to creating a successful strategy. Let's move on to step two.

STEP TWO: TAKE STOCK

SIZE UP THE PLAYERS ON YOUR TEAM
AND

SIZE UP THE PLAYERS ON THEIR TEAM

"Know the enemy and know yourself; in a hundred battles you will never be in peril.

When you are ignorant of the enemy but know yourself, your chances of winning or losing are equal.

If ignorant both of your enemy and of yourself, you are certain in every battle to be in peril."

Sun Tzu
The Art of War

Once you have determined the size and the shape of the environmental truck that is threatening you, and once you have discovered who the drivers are, you are finished with step one and you are ready for step two. It is time for you to take stock.

In order to have an effective strategy, you have to be able to clearly define the strengths and weaknesses of the players on the opposing team. I will suggest six actions you should take to determine how strong the players are on your team and how strong the players are on the opposing team. Then I will discuss each of these six actions in some detail.

How to Take Stock — Six Actions Suggested During Step Two

1. List your personal strengths and weaknesses as they relate to your specific environmental negotiation, and list your team's strengths and weaknesses.
2. List the strengths and weaknesses of the opposing team's leaders, and list the strengths and weaknesses of the opposing team as a whole.
3. Imagine potential allies that you might approach to help you. List important individuals and organizations who share a common interest with you during this particular environmental negotiation.
4. Imagine potential allies that your opponent might approach to help him. List the individuals and organizations who may share a common interest with him during this negotiation.
5. Add up the strengths and weaknesses of you and your team, and add up the strengths and weaknesses of the opposing team. Compare the strengths and weaknesses of your team with the strengths and weaknesses of the opposing team.
6. Imagine these three possible scenarios for your environmental negotiation. Imagine the best result possible, the worst result possible, and finally, the most likely result of your environmental negotiation.

Let me explain the necessity of taking these six actions before you begin your environmental negotiation. If you are going to war with someone, if you are competing with another team in an athletic contest, or if you are entering into an environmental negotiation with an opposing team, you have to know beforehand what resources your team can bring to bear on the situation. A quick and easy way to determine your team's assets is to take an inventory.

Start with yourself. What is your standing in the community? Do people like and respect you? Are you a primary leader? Do you understand the issue you are negotiating? Do you know how the environmental negotiation game is played? Can you state your concerns clearly and succinctly to others?

Expand your inventory to include the rest of your team. How many players are already on your team? How knowledgeable are they concerning the environmental issue that is being negotiated? How many primary leaders are there among your team members? Have any elected officials or bureaucrats indicated that they are willing to work with you? Does your team have any specialty players, such as engineers, lawyers, or lobbyists, that you can call upon when they are needed? What do the industrialists and the developers have to say about your issue? What about the environmental activists and the leading environmental organizations? Have they taken a position on your issue yet? Is the media covering your negotiation? Is the media helping or hurting your cause? What kind of media coverage do you anticipate receiving in the future? Have you found any translators or bridgebuilders who are willing to work with you?

It is not enough, of course, to know just your team's strengths and weaknesses. You also have to have a clear picture of the opposing team. You should do the same analysis concerning the opposing team that you did regarding your own. Ask the same kinds of questions concerning their players that you asked concerning yours.

Begin with the leaders of the opposing team. Analyze them as thoroughly as you analyzed yourself.

Next, consider the other players on the opposing team. How many primary leaders are supporting your opponent? How many politicians and bureaucrats are working with them? Does the opposing team have any engineers, lawyers, and lobbyists readily available? Are the industrialists, the developers, and environmental activists supporting your opponent? What kind of media coverage is the opposing team receiving?

Let us return to our hypothetical example of the neighborhood battling a proposed toxic-waste site. In this example, the first thing that both teams must do during this step is to take stock of their strengths and weaknesses.

First, Connie Kubiak has to take stock of her strengths and weaknesses, and of her team's strengths and weaknesses.

Connie decides that her greatest personal strength is her established reputation in her community for getting things done. She has a proven record of success in organizing community projects. Connie believes that she is creative, flexible, and persistent. She has the ability to work with all kinds of people. Connie knows that she is a leader who can motivate others.

Connie admits that she has several areas of weakness as an environmental negotiator. She has trouble delegating work to others. She lacks technical expertise and is not familiar with the environmental regulatory process. Connie has never before engaged in an environmental negotiation. She does not know the players, the rules of the game, strategy, or tactics.

As Connie examines her team, she finds that they have few strengths and many weaknesses. Her neighborhood is united in its opposition to the project, but the total number of residents is too small to be politically compelling. The neighborhood residents display occasional intense energy, but they lack direction. They are easily bored and distracted. They feel inadequate in the face of company experts. Connie will have difficulty maintaining the momentum and the financial support necessary to sustain opposition over time.

Professional expertise is available from outside the neighborhood, but the people are too poor to pay for that expertise. One key official from the metropolitan health department has indicated that he supports the neighborhood's position but all other regulatory agencies are indifferent, or they support the company. One metropolitan city councilmember, the local school board members, and a couple of city councilmembers from the small town closest to the proposed site are all on Connie's team. Most of the other elected officials in the area are noncommittal.

As the company leaders, Ivan Thicke and Erin Metall, take stock of their situation, they find that they have many strengths and few weaknesses. They both have advanced professional educations, they are politically well-connected, and they enjoy good reputations with their business and professional peers.

They realize that their chief personal weakness is that they are outsiders. They are not from the area where the facility is to be located, and the people in the area do not trust them for that reason. They face mounting opposition and are unable to diffuse it.

As they examine their team, Thicke and Metall believe they have great cause for optimism. The company's resources seem endless. The company has strong ties to financial investors. They are able to hire as many engineers, lawyers, and scientific experts as they need. The company has already received preliminary backing from the regulatory agencies that will be issuing the needed permits.

Once you have completed your inventory of your team and of your opponent's team, you should begin to imagine potential allies you could recruit to improve your team. You need allies to magnify your team's strengths, and you need allies to correct any serious deficiencies in your team.

The natural place to start looking for allies is among the people you know: your friends, your relations, your neighbors, your colleagues at work, the members of your church, and so forth. Put another way, the most likely place for you to begin looking for allies is among *the people who are like you* in one way or another.

It is fine to recruit people who are like you in order to strengthen your team. You can quickly expand the raw numbers of players on your team through this method. If you are a developer, you are comfortable asking other developers to be your allies. If you are an environmental activist, it is easy to ask other environmental activists to be on your team. If you are a civic club president, you have no problem asking other civic club presidents to support you in your negotiations.

Unfortunately, recruiting only those people who are like you makes for very limited success in environmental negotiations. If you are going to be a successful environmental negotiator on a grand scale, you have to expand your imagination. You have to consider as potential allies people you would not normally think of as being your kind of folks.

To address fundamental weaknesses in your team, you have to recruit allies who are different from you and from your other team members. If you only recruit people who are like you, you will severely limit your team's effectiveness and you will perpetuate your team's weaknesses.

Imagine for a moment that your environmental negotiating

team is a football team. On your team you have many small, fast, agile receivers, but you have no large, durable linemen. If you want to have a winning team, you have to recruit some people who are not like your current team lineup. You have to recruit some big, strong linemen.

It works the same way in environmental negotiations. If your environmental negotiating team is composed primarily of environmental activists, then you need to recruit some engineers, some politicians, and some industrialists to play on your team. If your team is made up mostly of engineers, you need to find some allies who are politicians, environmental activists, lawyers, and so forth. You are looking for allies who are different from you and your team because they bring new skills, new attributes, and new constituencies to your negotiating team.

You must not add new members to your team who are likely to be fundamentally opposed to the goals of your negotiation. The people you are seeking as allies can be different from you in many ways, but they must share a *common interest* with you in order to be dependable allies. You and your potential allies must have negotiating goals that are in both of your self-interests. Only if you share this common self-interest with your potential allies can you be reliable helpers for one another.

Your task as an environmental negotiator is to discover how your team's self-interest coincides with that of your potential ally. Sometimes the common self-interest is obvious. All you have to do is to articulate it to the person you are trying to recruit. Other times you have to use your skills as a negotiator to create a common interest, a shared benefit, between you and your would-be ally.

It is no secret that people are heavily motivated by self-interest. If you can discover, or create, an important common interest that you and your potential ally share on a particular issue, then you are well on your way to having a reliable ally.

While you are considering potential allies for yourself, remember to speculate on what kind of allies your opponent may be seeking. If he is like most people in the world, he will first look for help from individuals and from organizations who are just like him.

He may or may not be smart enough to look for allies who are different from him, but who share a common interest with him. Try to determine as early as possible in the negotiating process whether or not your opponent is going outside of his normal circle of friends to find allies.

Pray that he is not smart enough to go outside his regular circle. If he fails to recruit players who are different from him and from his other team members, he will fail to correct basic weaknesses in his team. You will be able to target those weaknesses, and to exploit them without mercy.

If he shows signs of actively recruiting people who are different, then you will certainly have your work cut out for you as an environmental negotiator. It will be much more difficult to estimate the ultimate strength of your opponent's team, and it will be a much more difficult challenge to design a successful strategy.

Let us return to the negotiation between Connie Kubiak and the toxic-waste company. Let us examine how Connie and the company developed their respective lists of potential allies.

First, let us begin with Connie and her neighborhood negotiating team. After reviewing their strengths and weaknesses, Connie and her team saw that they were too poor, and too weak, to approach higher political authorities immediately. They knew that they would need them as allies eventually, but they felt it would be better to gain allies using the "bottom-up" approach rather than the "top-down" approach. In other words, Connie and her team decided to build a foundation from the bottom, by targeting potential allies who had strong personal ties to the area surrounding the proposed toxic-waste site.

Relying on her knowledge of the community, Connie compiled a list of key community leaders that she wanted as allies. She imagined the leaders of area churches, the local school board members, the area business owners, the major property owners, the board members of nearby municipal utility districts, the leaders of volunteer fire and ambulance services, and the local civic clubs and property owners associations.

The neighborhood team wanted to expand its list to include environmental organizations and environmental experts in the metropolitan community who were likely to be sympathetic to its position. Using the phone book, Connie began calling various environmental and health listings. After a couple of weeks of conducting this type of research, she was able to expand her list of potential allies considerably. Her list now included a well respected environmental attorney, one metropolitan city councilmember, the top two officials of the metropolitan health department, a prominent environmental engineer, and professors from the School of Public Health. Several environmental organizations also appeared likely candidates for allies, including the Citizens for the Environment, Clean Water Now, the Toxic Task Force, the local Audobon Society, and the local Sierra Club.

While the neighborhood team decided to use the bottom-up approach, the company chose to use the top-down approach. Mr. Thicke and Mr. Metall felt that their deep pockets, their high standing in business and professional circles, and their formidable connections with politicians and regulatory personnel permitted them to approach the most powerful government officials directly.

They wanted to secure the support of high-ranking regulatory agency directors and bureaucrats. They would immediately approach key personnel at the Department of Energy, the Environmental Protection Agency, the state Air Control Board, and the state Water Commission.

After neighborhood opposition emerged, the company leaders believed that they needed the support of important local political leaders. Thicke and Metall determined that the most powerful person in the semi-rural area was the county judge. They put him first on their list of potential allies. Next, they added the names of the mayors of all of the surrounding towns, the members of the county commissioners court, and the various small town councilmembers.

They also decided that they needed the support of powerful local business interests. They added the names of the president of the local chamber of commerce, the president of the largest bank in the area, the wealthiest people living in the surrounding communities, the major property owners, and the owners of well-known local businesses.

They thought it would not be necessary to contact the local state legislators and the congressmen for the area. They felt their connections with regulatory agencies and with local government officials would be sufficient.

After you have speculated on your opponent's potential allies, you are ready for the fifth action in step two. You are ready to add up the total strengths and weaknesses of the two teams. When you total the strengths and weaknesses of your team, don't forget to add in the strengths and weaknesses of your likely allies. Add up the strengths and weaknesses of the opposing team. Don't forget to add in the strengths and weaknesses of your opponent's likely allies. Once you have completed your lists, compare your team's total assets and liabilities with the total assets and liabilities of your opponent's team.

As you compare, ask yourself some simple questions. Where is my team stronger than theirs? Do I have more people or greater expertise or better political connections or more money? Are the merits of the issue clearly in my favor? Am I intellectually quicker than my opponent? Am I more creative and more flexible as a negotiator?

Also confess to yourself those areas where your opponent's team is stronger than yours. Does his team have more players than your team? Are his players, on the whole, more skilled and more experienced than your players? Does his team have more professional expertise in certain areas, such as engineering and the law? Does he have more money than you? Are his pockets deeper than yours if the environmental negotiation becomes a war of attrition?

Returning to our toxic-waste site example, the neighborhood team and the company team prepared similar lists of strengths and weaknesses for themselves and for each other. Their lists looked like this:

Neighborhood Team	Company Team
Strengths	**Strengths**
1. Strong local support	1. Strong finances, deep pockets
2. Primary leader with proven reputation	2. Powerful political connections
3. One big-city council-member	3. Strong business and professionalreputations
4. Some small-town councilmembers	4. Professional education

Neighborhood Team	Company Team

Strengths (continued)

Neighborhood Team

5. Some local school board members

Company Team

Strengths (continued)

5. Limitless professional consulting services
6. Sympathetic regulatory agencies
7. Leaders familiar with regulatory process
8. Leaders understand environmental negotiations

Weaknesses

Neighborhood Team

1. Neighborhood poor — no money
2. Leader unfamiliar with regulatory process

3. Leader does not understand environmental negotiations.
4. Small neighborhood — not politically well-connected
5. Neighborhood people easily bored and frustrated
6. Leader not good at delegating responsibilities
7. Most politicians indifferent to neighborhood concerns

Company Team

Weaknesses

1. Unable to control neighborhood opposition
2. Leaders and company are perceived as outsiders

Once you have honestly compared your team to your opponent's, you are ready for the sixth and final action in step two. You are ready to imagine possible scenarios for your environmental negotiation.

First, imagine the best possible result you could hope to achieve through your environmental negotiation. What is the best end result you could hope for?

When you imagine the brightest and the best scenario, be realistic, but be optimistically realistic. Do not engage in idle fantasy, but do engage in some serious positive thinking. How good could it get?

Next, imagine the worst possible scenario for your environmental negotiation. What is the worst possible end result of your negotiation? How bad could it get?

When you imagine your worst case scenario, be realistic, but be pessimistically realistic. Don't go off the deep end. Don't indulge in suicidal imaginings, and don't go into an irreversible depression thinking about every single thing that could go wrong. You only want to imagine the worst possible scenario for a little while in order to give your thinking some structure and some balance before you enter into full-blown negotiations.

Finally, imagine the most likely scenario based on the information you have available at the time. Try to be as objective and as even-handed as you can be during your imagining of this scenario. You know the best that you could hope for, and you know the worst that could befall you. Now, what is the most likely way your environmental negotiation will go?

In the case of Connie and the neighborhood team, the best possible result would be for the company to fold up its tents, to leave the community, and to stay away. The worst possible scenario would be for the company to begin operating a toxic-waste facility in their community.

After studying the regulatory process in some detail, the neighborhood negotiating team believes that the most likely scenario is that the company will receive its preliminary permits, but will become bogged down during the public hearing process. They predict a war of attrition will ensue between the community and the company.

From the company's perspective, the best possible result would be to receive their permits promptly and to become an active toxic-waste facility at the site it selected. The worst possible scenario for the company would be investing a fortune in time and money in the project, slugging it out with the neighborhood through the entire regulatory process, and then not receiving the permits required to operate the facility.

After reviewing their situation, the leaders of the company decide that the most likely scenario is that they will receive their permits and begin operation of the toxic-waste facility after some delay due to neighborhood opposition.

When you have the most likely scenario, the most realistic scenario, firmly fixed in your mind, you are finished with step two. You are now ready for step three.

STEP THREE: ORGANIZE

DEVELOP YOUR GAME PLAN AND PREPARE YOUR TEAM

"It is time to put some walk to our talk."

Jim Hightower, former Texas Agriculture Commissioner

"'Would you tell me, please, which way I ought to go from here?'
'That depends a good deal on where you want to get to,' said the
Cat."

Alice's conversation with the Cheshire Cat in Wonderland

The first two steps of the environmental negotiation process, doing research and taking stock, make heavy use of your intellectual abilities. As you do research and take stock, you rely heavily on your skills at gathering, storing, and processing information. Certainly, good interpersonal skills are helpful as you conduct your investigation and as you analyze the facts you discover. Interpersonal skills are not the most important factor during step one and step two, however.

Your intellectual abilities, and the intellectual abilities of your team leaders, are the most important factors in completing steps one and two successfully. Steps one and two are introspective and personal experiences. Most of your work during these two steps is done by you alone, or by working with a small group of leaders.

As you move to step three, organizing, the emphasis and the focus shift. The skill requirements change substantially. While doing research and taking stock are introspective, intellectual actions that utilize your investigative and analytical skills, step three is an extrospective, interpersonal activity that tests your leadership talents and social skills.

The organizing step in environmental negotiations consists of six essential actions. I will list these six actions that make up step three. Then I will comment on each of the six actions, and I will make suggestions regarding each.

The Six Essential Actions for Organizing

1. Educate and mobilize the players already on your team.
2. Actively approach potential allies, and if they share a common interest with you, persuade them to join your team.
3. Educate and mobilize the allies you have successfully recruited.
4. Set realistic goals for your environmental negotiation.
5. Develop a specific plan of action. Include a timetable for each phase of your plan of action.
6. Delegate. Assign appropriate responsibilities to your teammates and to your allies. Let them know that the whole team will be counting on them to fulfill the tasks they have been assigned.

Let me elaborate a little on each of the six actions that make up step three. I will take up each of these actions one at a time.

Action Number One: Educate and mobilize the players already on your team

Educating and mobilizing the players on your team is an

obvious organizing necessity, but many environmental negotiators overlook these important actions. We all tend to assume that if someone is with us, that they know why they are with us. We believe that if they are on our side, that they understand the environmental issue that is being negotiated. Unfortunately, it is rarely the case that all the players on a given negotiating team know why they are on that team. It is rarer still when all the players on a team understand, with any thoroughness, the environmental issue that is being negotiated.

If your team members are going to be dependable partners in your environmental negotiation, they have to understand the issue. If they do not understand the issue, your job as an environmental negotiator is to teach them as much as you can about the issue at hand.

In the hypothetical toxic-waste facility example, Connie and the neighborhood team must educate themselves before they are ready to approach any potential allies. The community group meets to discuss their concerns, to share information obtained through research, and to focus on a few of the issues that they can understand quickly and easily. The team leader prepares a fact sheet describing the selected issues. The group is particularly concerned about (1) the unproven nature of salt-dome technology for the disposal of solidified toxic waste, (2) toxic air emissions, (3) the potential for water contamination, (4) the transportation of toxic materials through the neighborhood, and (5) the negative impact on property values.

The team members study the fact sheet to become familiar with the information it contains. If the team members have questions regarding the fact sheet, they ask the team leader for more information, and she does her best to respond. Once the team members are comfortable discussing the issues with each other, they feel more prepared to present the issues to potential allies.

The neighborhood team realizes that their concerns may take some time to address, so they organize a neighborhood-based, grass-roots environmental organization. The primary issue of the new environmental organization is the proposed toxic-waste facility. The new organization becomes identified as the leading opponent of the toxic-waste company; it becomes the organized mechanism for mobilizing the troops.

Once the team members understand the issues regarding the proposed toxic-waste facility, they share their newly acquired knowledge with their neighbors by word of mouth. They find that their neighbors are equally alarmed about the project and that their neighbors are ready to help fight the project.

The neighborhood team is now mobilized. They are ready to approach potential allies to see if those potential allies share a common interest with them.

The company is much further along than the neighborhood in terms of educating and mobilizing its players. Thicke, Metall, and the company team have been working on the toxic-waste project for nearly 10 years. They are already well-educated about the project.

Metall, the project engineer, is convinced that the project is sound from an engineering standpoint and that it will make a lot of money. Company employees are highly motivated because they believe they will receive great financial rewards if the project goes through. They are faithful to the company and they do as they are told.

Metall tells the company team that those in the community who are opposing the project do not have all of the facts and do not understand the nature of the project. He says that educating the public through the media will win all reasonable people over to the company's point of view. He believes that through the company team's educational efforts, the credibility of the neighborhood leaders will be dissolved.

The company leaders tell their team not to acknowledge that there is any opposition, because they do not want to alarm investors. The leaders announce that the company will respond quickly through the media to any negative publicity concerning the proposed toxic-waste facility. The company team makes sure its employees get the finest public relations training available and that they are well-coached on how to overcome the objections of the community.

The company has already started from a position of strength. They are educated, mobilized, and ready to approach potential allies. They are prepared to convince the potential allies that the public is too ignorant to know what is in its best interest.

Part of your job as an educator includes explaining the environmental negotiating process to the players on your team. They are not going to be helpful and effective players if they don't know how the game is played. It is a good idea for you to review with them the five steps in the environmental negotiating process: do research, take stock, organize, act, and react. Draw them a picture of where they are in the negotiating process at that given moment. Tell them what steps have been taken and what steps will be taken in the future.

Once you have thoroughly educated your team players, you are now ready to mobilize them. Let them know that they are on alert, that they need to be in a state of readiness. A serious encounter with the other side is about to take place. They need to be prepared to play the big game.

Action Number Two: Actively approach potential allies, and if they share a common interest with you, persuade them to join your team

When you were taking stock in step two, you were told to imagine potential allies who might share a common interest with you. Now that you are in step three, organizing, you need to stop imagining potential allies and to start recruiting real ones. The only way you will know if people are willing to be on your team is to go to them and to ask them.

Before you ask someone to play on your team, probe that individual to find out if you share a common interest with him. It is important for you to explain your concerns about a particular issue to a potential ally.

It is more important, however, for you to listen to a potential ally's concerns about that issue. Talk and listen, and listen and talk. You should never talk and talk and talk when you are trying to recruit an ally. If you fail to listen, you will not find out if he shares a common interest with you.

If you do not take the time to hear his concerns, you will not make a favorable impression on your potential friend. Everyone thinks that he has important, insightful things to say. Your potential ally will see you as being a wise person if you listen attentively to what he has to say. If you spend all of your time talking at him, he will view you as being an ignorant, arrogant individual who doesn't have the sense to listen to the words of wisdom he has to convey.

In our toxic-waste facility example, the neighborhood team first contacts the churches in the area. The neighborhood team asks the churches to remember the project in their prayers and to keep their memberships informed. The churches agree to announce the neighborhood team's public meetings and to distribute the team's project updates. Some of the churches view the potential environmental problems from the proposed toxic-waste site as being an example of poor stewardship of the Earth, and they become allies.

Next, the neighborhood leaders approach the two nearby school districts. The school district officials become concerned about the transportation of toxic waste while the children are traveling to and from school. Connie Kubiak, the primary leader, attends the school board meetings of these two school districts and asks each school board to pass a resolution opposing the toxic-waste facility. Both school boards vote unanimously to oppose the facility. The school board members send copies of their resolutions to all of the other elected officials who serve the area.

The neighborhood team makes an interesting discovery when they approach area business people and property owners. The smaller "mom and pop" business owners are very supportive of the neighborhood's position. The larger businesses refuse to take a position on the proposed facility. The area property owners are all opposed to the project, with one notable exception. That exception is the large property owner who is selling the company the land on which the toxic-waste operation would be located.

The small area businesses oppose the project because they are afraid that a toxic-waste facility in the neighborhood would drive people away. Most of the area property owners are against the company because they live in the area, their children attend local schools, and they drink water that could be contaminated by the project. The property owners are also concerned about the negative effects the facility could have on their property values.

The neighborhood team is gaining momentum. They are acquiring support from all kinds of places. Neighborhood people petition their municipal utility district board members. Every municipal utility district in the area goes on record in opposition to the project. Every volunteer fire department, every local civic club, and every property owners association in the area join the neighborhood team in opposing the toxic-waste facility. The neighborhood leaders gain strong support from several environmental organizations and from many environmental experts.

Connie Kubiak, the neighborhood leader, believes that the single most important potential ally could be the large metropolitan city government. Lake Blackburn is the largest single source of drinking water for that large city's residents; the lake would clearly be threatened by a toxic-waste facility in its watershed.

She persuades her team to ask the big-city councilmembers to oppose the project. After several months of delay in order to study the possible effects of the proposed facility, those city councilmembers vote to hire experts and to hire attorneys to fight the project.

While the neighborhood team is busy recruiting a wide variety of allies, the company team quickly and quietly secures allies: the county judge and the county commissioners, the mayor and several councilmembers from the nearby small town, high-ranking bureaucrats in regulatory agencies, the president of the local chamber of commerce, the president of the biggest area bank, and the largest landholder in the area. All agree to support the company's proposed toxic-waste facility.

Once you have determined that someone's self-interests are compatible with yours, forthrightly ask him to join your team. If he says no to you, move on to the next potential ally. It is seldom useful to debate, to argue, or to beg. Give it your best shot and move on.

Action Number Three: Educate and mobilize the allies you have successfully recruited

Just because you have persuaded someone to join your team doesn't mean he knows everything he needs to know to play on your team. Educate your new ally using the same techniques and the same approach you used to educate your original team members. Then mobilize your ally. Let him know that big things are about to happen in your environmental negotiation, and that he is going to be a big part of it.

The neighborhood team participating in the toxic-waste facility negotiation uses several techniques to educate and to mobilize its allies. The team believes that a petition drive will serve to educate the general public and to mobilize the troops. Petitions opposing the toxic-waste project are placed in churches, in "mom and pop" businesses, and in local schools. Signatures are gathered door to door throughout the neighborhood.

The neighborhood leaders hold a series of public meetings in the community to inform residents of the potential problems associated with the toxic-waste facility. The public meetings are also pep rallies designed to inspire the neighborhood residents to continue their fight against the proposed facility.

Periodically the neighborhood leaders contact the local papers to express their concerns and to report on new developments associated with the proposed project. Stories about the neighborhood's opposition to the project appear in the local papers almost every week. The leaders also give several TV and radio interviews concerning the facility.

To educate and to mobilize environmental organizations and environmental experts, the neighborhood team sends information packages containing the team's research findings. The packages describe the company's proposal in some detail; they also state the neighborhood's specific environmental and health concerns.

The company team educates and mobilizes its allies by demonstrating the economic benefits that the area will receive if the project becomes operational. The company team leaders promise that many new jobs will be created and that local people will be given preference in receiving those jobs. The company places major deposits in the largest local bank to inspire the bank's enthusiastic support. The company purchases livestock from local children who are members of the Future Farmers of America. As a result, the FFA children and their parents are mobilized to support the company.

The company team members mobilize the support of elected officials in a variety of ways. They buy a worthless tract of land from the small-town mayor and pay a premium price for it. The company leaders purchase a hunting and fishing lease from the county judge for property that offers no known hunting or fishing opportunities. They offer to buy the business of an important school board member.

The company team hires public relations experts to prepare slick color brochures and a $50,000 video describing the project and its many benefits to the area's economy. They present the brochures and the videos to elected officials and to key regulatory bureaucrats. They take out ads in the local newspaper offering free brochures and free videos to anyone who wants them.

Action Number Four: Set realistic goals for your environmental negotiation

You have finally reached the stage in the negotiating process where you are ready to define what you can reasonably hope to achieve through your environmental negotiation. It is time to set your goals. If you are this far along in the process, you probably have a pretty good notion of what you hope to accomplish through your negotiation that you could not achieve otherwise.

Now is the time for you to clarify those somewhat vague ideas you have. In specific, concrete terms, what do you want to do? A useful way to flesh out your goals is to try to express those goals to your team players. If you can state your goals clearly and concisely to your teammates, then you probably know where you want to go with your negotiation. If it takes you a half an hour or more to state you goals, then you probably have a lot more clarifying to do.

When you are goal-setting, remember to ask the other team members what their goals are. As they present to you their goals for the negotiation, they become clearer. As you present your goals to them, you become clearer. As you share your goals with each other, you and your colleagues begin to develop momentum and team spirit. It is in establishing group goals that you and your fellow players really become a team.

You and your team members need to establish two kinds of goals: short-term, practical goals and long-term, inspiring goals. You need to have both kinds of goals. The practical, short-term goals are the nuts-and-bolts objectives that you are trying to accomplish in this specific negotiation. The long-term, inspiring goals that you establish will probably not be achieved during your immediate negotiation, but they will act as a shared vision that pull you and your team forward.

Apply the test of practicality to all of your group's goals, but be sure to end up with some goals that are truly inspiring. Your team's goals will be your focus and your rallying point during all of the long and trying work that lies ahead. You will need to have some goals that inspire you and your players. If some of your goals are not magnets that pull you onward, then work on your goals.

You must set short-term, practical goals for your specific environmental negotiation, but it is useful for you to realize that specific, immediate negotiations can have long-term consequences and benefits as byproducts. You need to look beyond the immediate negotiation to where you want to be as an environmental negotiator in the future.

If you are having trouble establishing long-term, inspiring goals, let me make the following suggestions. One of your long-term goals should be to strengthen your position as an environmental negotiator. You will certainly have other environmental negotiations in the future. It is a good idea to remember that you want to come out of the current negotiation in an improved condition to win those future environmental negotiations. Plan ways to preserve and to perpetuate your team. Think of other environmental issues that you and your team can work on together in the future.

In our toxic-waste facility negotiation, these are some of the goals that Connie Kubiak and the neighborhood team establish for themselves.

Short-Term, Practical Neighborhood Goals

1. Unite the community in opposition to the proposed project.
2. Establish credibility with the media, with the regulatory agencies, and with the elected officials.
3. Scrutinize the company's permit applications and be prepared to challenge them.
4. Obtain as allies political officials who will publicly support the neighborhood team at the permit hearings.
5. Defeat the company's permit applications.

Long-Term, Inspiring Neighborhood Goals

1. Preserve the quality of life in the area.

2. Protect the health and safety of the people who live there, especially the children.
3. Defeat the company so decisively that no other company would attempt to locate a toxic-waste facility in the area.
4. Change state laws so that other communities would not have to face the threat of toxic-waste facilities in their neighborhoods.

The company team has set these goals for the environmental negotiation.

Short-Term, Practical Company Goals

1. Establish credibility with the community and with the media.
2. Maintain credibility with the regulatory agencies and with the elected officials.
3. Diffuse neighborhood opposition to the project.
4. Obtain as allies political officials who will publicly support the company team at the permit hearings.
5. Win permit approvals without excessive delay.

Long-Term, Inspiring Company Goals

1. Build and operate a successful toxic-waste facility at the selected site, so that the company will have an easier time opening this type of facility at other locations.
2. Make a strong profit at the proposed facility so that company investors will want to finance future toxic-waste projects of this type.

Be aware of the limitations of your players and of yourself as you go through the negotiations at hand. Make addressing those shortcomings one of your short-term, practical goals.

Be aware of your mistakes as you proceed through the current negotiation. One of your goals should be not to repeat those same mistakes in other environmental negotiations. It is normal to make mistakes in negotiations and in life, but it is foolish and unnecessary to make the same mistakes over and over. I am not telling you to be perfect. I'm telling you to make different mistakes as you participate in more and more environmental negotiations.

A final word on short-term, practical goals versus long-term, inspiring goals. You must have short-term, practical goals in order to accomplish the tasks at hand in the immediate negotiation. You have to know specifically what you want to accomplish in that specific negotiation. But you also need long-term, inspiring goals to help you to get through the current negotiation and to energize you for future negotiations. Long-term goal setting is the time and the place in the negotiating process to exercise your hopes and your ideals. Every goal you set should be grounded in reality, but long-term goal setting is also an opportunity for you to state your dreams.

Action Number Five: Develop a specific plan of action for your environmental negotiation. Include in your plan of action a timetable for each phase of your plan of action

You have your players educated and mobilized. You know your team's strengths and weaknesses. You know the opposing team's strengths and weaknesses. You have successfully recruited allies to play on your team. You have established short-term, practical goals and long-term, inspiring ones. Now you are ready to spell out the step-by-step details that will enable you to achieve those goals.

You are ready to create your team's game plan for the environmental negotiation, and you are ready to establish a timetable for executing that game plan. Let me describe for you how I go about establishing a plan of action with a timetable.

The central focus of your plan of action is your list of short-term goals. Take your list of short-term goals and rank each of them in the two following ways.

First, rank each of your short-term goals in terms of the goal's importance to you and to your team. Place the most important goal of your negotiation at the top of your list. Place the next most important goal below the first goal listed and so on. Rank every one of your short-term goals for the environmental negotiation in terms of its importance to you and to your team.

Then make another list that is the ranking of your short-term goals in terms of their relative degree of difficulty. Put at the top of the new list the easiest goal for you to achieve through your negotiation. Directly under it list the next easiest goal, and so on, until you have listed the most difficult short-term goal at the bottom of the new list.

Now take the first list, the list of your goals in terms of their relative importance, and compare it with your second list, the list of your goals in terms of their degree of difficulty. Identify goals that rank high in importance and high in ease of achievement. Your plan of action should target these kinds of goals.

Design a plan of action that begins with goals that are important and that are easy to achieve. There are two reasons for placing this type of goal at the beginning stages of your plan of action. The first reason is the fact that you don't want to spend your time on relatively unimportant goals until your more important goals have been addressed. The second reason is that in order for your team to establish momentum and a winning attitude, you need to experience early success. If you go after the most difficult goals at the beginning of your plan of action, you and your team could fail to achieve those goals and become discouraged. If you start with the easier goals, you and your team will almost certainly experience some initial success. That early success will give you and your team new energy, greater confidence, and a sense of building momentum.

Once you have discovered those goals that are relatively easy and relatively important, take each of these goals and break them into discreet, bite-sized pieces. What individual events need to occur in order to accomplish each individual goal? Decide which of the bite-sized chunks need to be accomplished first, second, and third. In other words, establish priorities for achieving the discreet pieces of each goal.

Imagine which of your players would be most suitable for handling each of the bite-sized chunks. Decide who has the personality, the skills, and the training to best perform the various tasks that need to be done to reach each goal.

Finally, do not forget to establish a timetable for achieving your goals and for performing the separate pieces of work that must be done to achieve these goals. A timetable is essential for every plan of action. It imposes discipline and structure on you and on your negotiating team. Some people feel that timetables trap and imprison them. The opposite is the case. A timetable frees you to do the things you most want to do. A timetable concentrates your actions, and it empowers you to eliminate distractions from your work. Time is a precious and profoundly limited resource. A timetable compels you to budget your time, and it urges you to use your time wisely.

Your timetable and your plan of action are wonderful tools you can use to see how you are doing. If things are going well, your timetable and your plan of action are powerfully encouraging. If things are not progressing as planned, your timetable and your plan of action are bold-faced challenges to get to work.

Connie Kubiak and the neighborhood team establish this plan of action and this timetable for the toxic-waste negotiation.

Neighborhood Action Plan with Timetable

1. Unite the community using petition drives, community meetings, and media appearances. Have the petition drive completed within 6 months. Hold community meetings each month until the permit hearings begin, 8 months from now. Put articles in local newspapers every week until the hearings. Give radio and TV interviews as often as possible.
2. Establish credibility with the media, the regulatory agencies, and the elected officials by giving them calm, factual, polite briefings on the problems associated with the proposed project. Media briefings begin immediately and continue until the hearing. Submit technical data revealing deficiencies in the project to the appropriate regulatory agencies during the 4 month review period. Have briefings with elected officials immediately, and schedule follow-up meetings as the need arises. Have every important elected official briefed no later than 2 months before the hearing.
3. Have friendly experts scheduled to challenge the company's permits at the hearings. Have all expert witnesses lined up no later than a month before the hearings begin.
4. Schedule supportive elected officials to contest the company permit applications at the public hearings. Have all elected officials who will testify scheduled no later than 1 month before the hearing.
5. Produce overwhelming technical evidence and demonstrate overpowering political strength at the hearings. Defeat the company permits. Defeating the permits will take anywhere from 6 months to 2 years after the hearings start.

6. Develop a plan of action for achieving long-term goals after the hearings are over and after the permits are defeated.

The company team establishes this plan of action and this timetable for its toxic-waste facility negotiation.

Company Action Plan with Timetable

1. Gain community acceptance by being generous, personable, corporate good neighbors. Continue making substantial donations to youth activities, to senior citizens programs, to community events, and to local chamber of commerce functions. Begin these donations immediately and continue until the permits are approved. Start distributing project brochures and videos to the media immediately. Make certain all relevant media outlets have received them within the first week of distribution.

2. Send teams of experts to the regulatory agencies to answer any objections raised by the agencies or by the opposition. The experts should begin visiting the regulatory agencies immediately; they should continue to return to the agencies regularly until the permits are granted. Have company leaders, Thicke and Metall, visit elected officials to solicit their support for the project at the upcoming hearings. All relevant elected officials should be visited no later than 3 months before the hearings begin.

3. Have company experts scheduled to appear at the hearings to refute any opposition to the permit applications. Have all company expert witnesses scheduled no later than 3 months before the hearings start.

4. Schedule elected officials who support the project to testify at the hearings. Have all elected officials who will testify for the company scheduled no later than 3 months before the hearings.

5. Produce overwhelming technical evidence and demonstrate overpowering political strength at the hearings. Receive the necessary permits no more than 6 months after the hearings commence.

6. Develop a company plan of action for achieving long-term goals after the permits are acquired.

Action Number Six: Delegate. Assign appropriate responsibilities to your teammates and to your allies. Let them know that the whole team will hold them accountable for fulfilling the tasks they have been assigned

You have heard the old saying, "If you want a job done right, do it yourself." What a bunch of nonsense! No one makes any progress in an environmental negotiation of any consequence alone. To be successful, an environmental negotiator needs a team composed of many different types of players. A successful environmental negotiating team must have all kinds of players with all types of talents, personalities, and constituencies. The motto of the environmental negotiator must be, "If you want a job done right, find the right people and get them to do it."

Earlier in this book I discussed the players of the game. Every type of player suffers from certain chronic liabilities, but each kind of player also has several redeeming assets. Use the special talents of each player to perform the various tasks required to reach your goals.

Here are some quick suggestions. Engineers can help you by designing technologically sound solutions to specific environmental problems that arise in the course of your negotiation. Politicians are skillful in channeling political power and in articulating issues to the media. Bureaucrats understand the rules and the machinery of government. Bureaucrats can be effective allies if your team needs to obtain information from government, or if you need to have the cooperation of governmental agencies to achieve your goals. Industrialists and developers are capable of skillfully addressing economic questions. Environmental activists can forcefully state an issue in terms of its environmental merits. They can also suggest ideal solutions to various environmental problems. Ordinary people are masters at articulating their own self-interests. Lawyers are excellent battering rams who can break down the opposing team, and lobbyists are marvelously skillful at seducing the opposing team members. The media has the unique ability to give shape and substance to issues. Translators, primary leaders, and bridgebuilders have the abilities to make complex issues comprehensible, to motivate people to action, and to bring about agreement.

Connie Kubiak and the neighborhood team delegate responsibilities in the following ways. Three separate committees made up of community people are established to handle three areas of responsibility: the petition drives, the monthly community meetings, and media relations. Connie remains the main spokesperson for the organization, but she delegates some of the interviews to leaders of supportive environmental organizations and to friendly experts.

The experts are given the responsibility of presenting the technical data required by the regulatory agencies. These experts agree to present objections to the permit applications at the upcoming permit hearings.

Connie forms a committee composed of business leader allies; she gives this committee the task of contacting all appropriate elected officials. She usually accompanies the business leaders committee when they meet with elected officials, but she permits the business leaders to be active participants in these briefings.

All the important elected officials agree to publicly support the neighborhood team's position at the permit hearings. They inform Connie that they will arrange their schedules in order to speak at the hearings.

The company delegates its responsibilities as well. The company gives Thicke carte blanche to make charitable contributions to any community causes that he selects. The public relations consultants are assigned the job of blanketing the media with the company brochures and videos.

Company technical experts are prepared to swarm all over the regulatory agencies. They are scheduled to offer testimony or rebuttal at the upcoming hearings.

Thicke and Metall visit key elected officials, but they discover that no elected officials are willing to speak on the company's behalf at the public hearings. The company leaders are disappointed, but they are able to persuade two powerful elected officials to stay away from the hearings altogether.

As an environmental negotiator, you have to assign appropriate responsibilities to each of these kinds of players. Never presume that they know what their job assignments are in your particular environmental negotiation. You have to spell out their assignments for them. You must make it clear to your players what you expect of them.

You have to make it clear to every player what his responsibilities are, and you have to let each player know that the whole team expects him to fulfill his responsibilities. It is often helpful to explain to a player exactly how his particular work assignment is an essential part of reaching the team's goals.

It is not necessary to be threatening. It is necessary to be clear and emphatic. Each player's job is important. The whole team is counting on every player to perform his assigned task. The team and the environmental negotiation are depending on him.

STEP FOUR: ACT

"Action is a lack of balance. In order to act you must be somewhat insane. A reasonably sensible man is satisfied with thinking."

George Clemenceau, 1928

"Organizations need action as an individual needs oxygen."

Saul Alinsky

The late Saul Alinsky, the godfather of all community organizers, said, "Organizations need action as an individual needs oxygen." Alinsky believed that a community organization needed action to stay alive, just as the body required oxygen to maintain life. Action was not an optional matter for Saul Alinsky, it was an absolute necessity.

Saul Alinsky's words are true for community organizations, and they are true for environmental negotiating teams. Sooner or later, you and your negotiating team have to act in order to keep your vitality. The first three steps in the negotiating process are worthwhile, *if they lead to action*.

Conversely, all the other steps in the negotiating process are almost meaningless if they don't lead to action. You can perform brilliant research on your issue. You can very thoroughly take stock of your team's strengths and weaknesses, and you can accurately assess the strengths and weaknesses of the opposing team. You can recruit powerful allies. You can educate your team members and your allies, and you can mobilize them. You can establish practical goals and inspiring ones. You can set a workable timetable. But, all of your efforts, and all of your team's efforts, will count for nothing if you fail to act.

Now you may be a little confused about what I mean by acting, since I have stressed the active nature of the three steps leading to step four: act. The explanation is simple.

Step four is the step in which you and your team engage the opposing team in a contest of wills to determine who wins the environmental negotiation. The first three steps in the negotiating process are tools that you use to prepare for this contest of wills.

To use a sports analogy, steps one through three are the practices and the preparation that an athletic team does in order to be ready for the big game. Step four: act is the big game.

Environmental negotiations are often different from sporting events, however, because a negotiating team usually has some flexibility regarding when it will play the big game with the opposing team. Sports teams have set schedules. Environmental negotiating teams can sometimes set their own schedules.

Environmental negotiations also differ from sporting events in that an environmental negotiating team often has the ability to decide where the contest of wills will take place. Environmental negotiating teams can frequently determine where the big game will be played.

Finally, environmental negotiators are sometimes able to select the opposing players with whom they will negotiate. Sports coaches, of course, do not have this kind of option. A basketball coach cannot say to the opposing coach, "I will play your team only if you agree to use the five players who I select from your team." Believe it or not, in environmental negotiations, you, the environmental negotiator, occasionally have the power to do just that. You sometimes can decide who your team will play against in the contest of wills, in the big game.

Environmental negotiators have three choices to make that athletic coaches rarely have to make. Environmental negotiators must decide:

1. When will my team and I engage the opposing team in a contest of wills? When will we play the big game with the opposing team?
2. Where will this contest of wills take place? In what forum, in what location, will we play the big game?
3. Who will my opponents be in this contest of wills? Which of the players from the opposing team will we choose to negotiate with? Which specific opposing team players will we agree to play in the big game?

Let us examine the three basic questions regarding action: *when to act, where to act, and against whom to act.* Answering each of these three questions will give you a solid strategic basis for effective action.

Question Number One Regarding Action: When will my team and I engage the opposing team in a contest of wills?

There are three mistakes you can make concerning when to engage the opposing team in a contest of wills. You can act too soon, you can act too late, and you can fail to act at all.

The third mistake, failing to act at all, is the most common. I do not fully understand the reasons for this fact, but I certainly can describe the characteristics that accompany failure to act.

The typical negotiating team that fails to act is always planning some future action. It spends hours and hours in internal debate and reflection, searching for the perfect time to act, the perfect place to act, and the perfect opponent to act against. For a while, this type of team enjoys the endless planning, reflection, and debate.

This kind of negotiating team eventually runs out of time and out of energy before it does anything, however. The team dies before it acts. More to the point, the team dies because it fails to act.

If you are the leader of an environmental negotiating team that seems consumed by endless planning, reflection, and internal debate, I give you this advice. Forget about finding the perfect time to act. The perfect time for you to act does not exist, just as the perfect negotiating team does not exist. If it is any comfort to you, be clear that there is no perfect time for the opposing team to act either.

Your environmental negotiating team may lose if you try to play the big game too early or too late, but your team will certainly lose if you forfeit the big game by failing to show. I am proud of you for performing the first three steps in the negotiating process. All of that research and taking stock and organizing will serve you well when the big-time action starts. I am proud of you for establishing team goals and for setting a team timetable. Now that you have established your goals, go after them! You have set your timetable, follow it!

Your team may die if you repeatedly fail to win, but it will certainly die if you fail to engage the opposing team in a major contest of wills. Execute your plan of action and take your chances.

"All right, all right," you tell me. "Enough preaching about failing to act. What about the other two mistakes, acting too soon and acting too late? How do I avoid making those mistakes?" you ask.

These questions are difficult to answer. I freely admit that properly timing your actions is an inexact science. Circumstances vary with each environmental negotiation. I cannot give you hard and fast rules about when to act. I cannot give you rules that will apply equally well to all types of environmental negotiations. All too often, you will learn whether you acted too soon or too late only after the fact. Although I cannot give you binding rules, I can give you some guidelines, some useful questions you can ask yourself when you are contemplating when to act.

If you are wondering whether or not it is the right time to act, ask yourself the following questions:

(1) *Have I completed steps one through three in the environmental negotiation process?* Never engage in a contest of wills until you have done your research, until you have taken stock of your team and of your opponent's team, and until you have properly organized your team and your allies.

On the other hand, do not use steps one through three as an excuse not to act. Perform steps one through three, and then act. Don't get stuck performing steps one through three over and over without taking action.

(2) *Is your team ready and at its peak?* Ask yourself if your team is as ready as it reasonably can be. Are your players focused on the task at hand? Are you attentive to your environmental negotiation, or are you distracted by other matters?

If you or your team members are lacking motivation or focus, use the goals you established to motivate you and your team, and to bring you all into sharper focus. Finally, and most importantly, ask yourself if further delays in acting would strengthen or weaken your team. If delaying action would strengthen your team, then you should probably wait awhile to act. If delays in acting would weaken your team, then you should almost certainly act immediately.

(3) *Do you have the opposing team's attention enough to negotiate with them?* You cannot engage in an environmental contest of wills by yourself. You cannot negotiate with yourself. You have to have the other team's attention in order to take meaningful actions.

If the opposing team is purposely ignoring you and your team, you have to develop the plans and the tactics necessary to get them to abandon that approach. You have to design a way to make it too costly for them to continue ignoring you. A critical feature of any action is the opposing team's reaction. Make sure you have enough of the opposing side's attention to cause them to react to you.

Many environmental negotiations allow room to maneuver regarding when the big game will be played. In our specific hypothetical example of the neighborhood opposing the company's toxic-waste facility, there is little opportunity for either side to affect when the big game will be played. Both the neighborhood and the company have decided that it is useless to negotiate with each other. The two opposing sides have chosen instead to negotiate with a third party, the regulatory agencies.

The regulatory agencies establish the rhythm of the negotiation, and the agencies set the timing of the permit hearings. Everyone involved in the negotiation — the neighborhood team, the company, and the regulatory agencies — realizes that the permit hearings are the big game. The outcome of the permit hearings determines the outcome of the toxic-waste facility negotiation.

The regulatory agencies check their books of rules and regulations. They are told by their rules that the permit hearings will begin 8 months after the company has submitted its permit application. Since everyone knows the date that the company submitted the permit applications, everyone knows when the permit hearings will take place.

Both the neighborhood team and the company team plan to be at the peak of readiness the day the hearings begin. Both teams focus their attention on getting prepared for the permit hearings.

Question Number Two Regarding Action: Where will this contest of wills take place?

Military strategists and historians devote a great deal of time to analyzing how location, climate, and terrain affect the outcomes of major battles. These factors can prove to be decisive in the contests of war. They can also be decisive in a contest of wills. Environmental negotiators should carefully consider the "where" question when they are planning a major engagement with the opposing team.

There are three "where" questions that you need to answer before choosing a location for the big game with the opposing team. The first question relates to convenience:

(1) *Is the location convenient for your team?* You want to select the location that causes your team the least expenditures of time, energy, and money. For example, you and your team may be able to require a government agency to hold a public hearing on a particular environmental issue.

That agency may offer to hold the hearing at one of three locations: the downtown area of your town, the state capital 200 miles from your town, or a place in your neighborhood. If your environmental issue is primarily a concern of the people in your neighborhood, you would want to hold the public hearing in your neighborhood. If your environmental issue affects everyone in your city and you expect to draw supporters from all over town, then the downtown location would be a good choice. The state capital location would be an unlikely choice, unless you really expect to draw supporters and allies from throughout the state.

You understand how you save time, energy, and money by holding the hearing either in downtown or in your neighborhood rather than in the state capital.

The second "where" question deals with how a given location affects your team politically and psychologically:

(2) *Is the location supportive of your team?* You want to select a location that is politically and psychologically supportive of your team. You want the big game to be played in front of the hometown crowd. You want to engage your opponent in a contest of wills in a place where the people love your position and hate your opponent's. It is a great feeling to receive cheers every time you open your mouth. It is also a great feeling to hear spontaneous boos emerge from the audience every time your opponent opens his mouth. The crowd reactions are particularly important if you and your opponent are competing in front of a neutral third party, such as a board or commission.

The political and psychological benefits of playing before a hometown crowd are enormous. It is a great confidence builder for you and your team. More subtle, but still extremely significant, is the effect the hometown crowd has on those neutral third parties. They find themselves moving away from neutrality and towards pleasing the hometown crowd.

Let me give you another example. It may be that your environmental problem could be solved either by city government action or by state government action. If the city government is sympathetic to your point of view, but the state government is not, try to stage your big battles with the opposing team at city hall.

Go to the place where the political climate is most supportive of your point of view. Use the political forum that is most sympathetic and least intimidating. Fight the big fights and play the big games where you and your team members feel comfortable, where the political climate agrees with you. That is where you will achieve the greatest success in your environmental negotiation.

The third "where" question describes how a location relates to your team's strengths and weaknesses:

(3) *Does the location minimize your team's weaknesses and maximize*

your team's strengths? The best examples for illustrating this type of question come from baseball. It is a common, and completely legal, practice for baseball teams to create home field advantages by adjusting the distances from home plate to the outfield fence. For instance, if a particular team has many home-run hitters, then that team will move their fence closer to home plate in order to maximize the benefits of that particular team strength. If a team does not have many long-ball hitters, the practice is to move the outfield fence as far away from home plate as legally possible in order to minimize that team weakness.

In environmental negotiations, you want to select a site that is tailored to suit your team's strengths and weaknesses. If your team is skilled at bureaucratic rules and regulations, try to have your contest of wills on bureaucratic turf. If your team has a large number of players, but your players have limited sophistication, try to imagine a political playing field where raw numbers are more important than the players' skill levels. Big rallies at public hearings immediately come to mind. If your team has a small number of players, but your players are very knowledgeable and very skillful, you can use media debates to emphasize your team's knowledge and skill. Media debates also compensate for your team's weakness, few players.

In our hypothetical toxic-waste facility negotiation, the issue of where the permit hearings will be held becomes critically important. The regulatory agencies allow the hearings to be held in the local community or in the state capital, 200 miles away. The regulatory agencies prefer to hold the hearings in the state capital, but their rules require them to hold the permit hearings in the affected local community if it appears that a large number of people are going to contest the permits.

The neighborhood discovers the rule requiring local hearings if the permits are contested. They quickly decide that they must persuade the regulatory agencies to hold the hearings in their neighborhood.

The neighborhood team has several reasons for believing it is in its best interest to have the hearings held locally:

1.   A local hearing is more convenient for the low-income residents of the neighborhood.

2.   It is a huge political and psychological advantage to have the hearings held in a friendly, local environment.

3.   A local hearing maximizes the neighborhood team's greatest strength, the ability to turn out large numbers of people.

The neighborhood team will be able to generate large numbers of people to attend the hearings if they are held close by. They will also find it easier to get the elected officials to keep their commitments to speak against the project. The elected officials are anxious to perform in front of the hometown folks.

Holding the hearings locally will also compensate for the neighborhood team's two greatest weaknesses: lack of sophistication concerning the regulatory process and lack of money. If the hearings are held in town, sympathetic local experts will provide their services for free. If the neighborhood's experts have to travel, they expect to receive compensation for at least the travel expenses. Having the hearings in town also eliminates the need to pay the neighborhood people's travel expenses. The neighborhood team does not have the resources to pay for either one of these expenses; holding the hearings locally neatly solves both potential problems.

The company team really wants the hearings to be held in the state capital. They certainly have valid reasons for thinking it is to their advantage to have the hearings take place in the state capital:

1.   With its deep pockets, the company is very mobile. It can go anywhere. It can retain lawyers and other experts in the state capital if necessary, or it can transport its lawyers and its experts to the state capital if it chooses. The company can transport as many company leaders and as many company witnesses to the state capital as it wishes. The company realizes that the neighborhood team does not have the same degree of mobility.

2.   The company team realizes that local hearings would be held under extremely hostile conditions. It is terrifying for the company to think about going into the community where the toxic-waste facility would be located to have the permit hearings. The political and psychological stress would be enormous. The company feels that the environment will be much friendlier in the state capital. Company leaders have extensive political connections in the state capital, and they are skilled at bureaucratic rules and regula-

tions. Having the hearings on the bureaucratic turf of the state capital suits the company just fine.

A battle ensues between the neighborhood team and the company team over where the hearings will take place. The neighborhood wants the hearings held locally, and the company wants the hearings held in the state capital. Each side attempts to persuade the regulatory agencies that the hearings should be held in the location that each of them prefers.

The neighborhood wages an aggressive campaign to convince the regulatory agencies to hold the hearings locally. They conduct a letter-writing campaign to demonstrate the magnitude of neighborhood opposition. Several hundred people write letters to regulatory agencies; they send copies of their letters to their state representatives and state senators. The state representatives, state senators, and even a member of the United States Congress agree to send letters of their own to the regulatory agencies asking that the hearings be held locally.

The company quietly lobbies the regulatory agencies urging them to hold the hearings in the state capital. The company leaders go to the state capital with their attorneys to talk directly to the regulators. The regulators are sympathetic to the company's point of view; it would be more convenient for the regulators to have the hearings held in the state capital.

The regulators study the situation, and they refer to their books of rules. Bureaucrats are not known for their flexibility or for their creativity, but they are known for following the rules. The regulators are aware of raw political power. They try to determine which way the political wind is blowing and act accordingly. After studying their rules, and after testing the political winds, the regulators decide that the hearings must be held in the community where the toxic-waste facility would be located.

Once you have successfully answered these three "where" questions, you are ready to answer the "who" questions. You are ready to decide, to the maximum extent possible, who your opponents will be in your environmental negotiations.

Question Number Three Regarding Action: Who will my opponents be in this contest of wills?

I realize that you do not always get to choose the opposing team members with whom you will negotiate. The leader of the opposing team wants to put his strongest players on the field. That may or may not suit your purposes. The important thing for you to remember is that you often do have some flexibility regarding which opposing players you ultimately engage in the contest of wills.

Where circumstances permit, try to select the negotiating opponent who is most conducive to your success. There are four "who" questions that you can utilize in determining the best possible negotiating opponent.

The first "who" question addresses your opponent's ability to help you meet your goals:

(1) *Who has the power to give you what you want?* There is no point at all, there is no benefit at all, in negotiating with someone who does not have the power to give you what you want. Engaging in a contest of wills with an opponent who cannot give you what you want is utterly useless and frustrating. Even if you win, you lose, because nothing happens.

Large organizations, especially large corporations and large governmental agencies, will send forth legions of public relations experts "to negotiate" with you. You could spend hours, days, weeks, and months in a protracted contest of wills with these public relations types only to discover that none of them had the real power to negotiate for the organizations they represent.

Before you decide to play someone in a big game, make certain that the outcome of the game really matters. It really matters if the players you are competing against have the power to give you what you want. The outcome of the game does not matter if the opposing team's players don't have the power to give you what you want.

Therefore, negotiate only with the opposing team's leaders, preferably their primary leaders. Primary leaders have real constituencies, real credibility, and real power. Avoid negotiating with public relations types. They rarely have any real power.

The second "who" question has to do with the negotiating skills of your opponent:

(2) *Who has the creativity to meet your goals and still look good himself?* Creativity is a gift from God. Some people have it. Most do not. If at all possible, try to negotiate with leaders who are capable of creative thinking. Most environmental contests of will are structured such that one side wins and the other side loses. Most people view environmental negotiation as a process in which if their team wins the other team must necessarily lose. It doesn't always have to be that way.

A creative negotiator can often think of solutions that permit both sides to claim a substantial measure of victory. A really skilled, really creative negotiator can figure out ways to give you what you want, while making certain that he looks good doing it.

You know you will be a creative negotiator. You will search for common interests that you and your negotiating opponent share. You will be open to solutions that allow both sides to get what they want, solutions that allow both sides to be winners. But you also understand that your life as a negotiator would be a lot easier and more successful if you could find a negotiating opponent who is also committed to the same approach.

Search for leaders on the opposing team who demonstrate creativity, and make every effort to negotiate with them. Try to avoid negotiating with those who see every gain for your team as a loss for theirs. Life is not always that rigid and that simplistic, but a person has to have creativity to be able to see it any other way.

The third "who" question relates to the personality of your opponent:

(3) *Who has the flexibility required to play the game?* One of the hallmarks of a bad environmental negotiation is a lack of flexibility on both sides. Negotiations are, by nature, give-and-take endeavors. The negotiating process implies movement, movement by both sides.

I am told that John Kennedy was frustrated by the inflexibility shown by the Soviets in his negotiations with them. He reportedly said that the Soviets' philosophy seemed to be "what's mine is mine, and what's yours is negotiable."

You are foolish to negotiate with an opponent who has the above philosophy, if you have the option of negotiating with someone who is willing to be more flexible. Search for players on the opposing team who demonstrate flexibility. Try to conduct your negotiations with them.

By the way, flexibility and creativity are often married. A creative personality is usually a flexible one, and vice versa. If you find an opponent who is flexible, he probably will appreciate your more creative approaches to environmental problem-solving.

The fourth "who" question asks which player on the opposing team is most predisposed to your point of view:

(4) *Who is most likely to give you what you want?* "Who" question number four is the bottom-line question that every environmental negotiator must ask himself. The answer to this question is reached by successfully answering the other three "who" questions.

This question contains a very simple truth that many negotiators overlook. That truth is that some opponents are much more likely to give you what you want than others. Some opponents are more powerful, more creative, more flexible, and more sympathetic to your point of view.

As an environmental negotiator, you will not always have the luxury of selecting the opponent with whom you will negotiate. Sometimes you will have to negotiate with adversaries who are dense, inflexible, and hostile. Sometimes there is no other alternative.

Yet, more often than you may realize, you *do* have the power to choose who your negotiating opponent will be. Frequently, you have the leeway to choose to negotiate with some players and to refuse to negotiate with others.

It is rarely a good idea to let the opposing team know that you are selecting your negotiating opponent. Their pride, ego, and need to feel in control require a great deal of subtlety on your part in choosing your negotiating opponent.

You may know in advance of the negotiation who you prefer as an opponent; or you may not discover your preferred negotiating opponent until you are in the heat of the contest. In either case, adjust your negotiating strategy by going after your preferred negotiating partner, the one who is most likely to give you what you want.

Three basic questions must be answered before an environmental negotiator acts: *when to act, where to act, and against whom to act.* In the toxic-waste site example, the first two questions have been answered. Now the third question must be addressed. Against whom do the two opposing sides act? To put the question another way, with whom will the two opposing teams agree to negotiate?

Early in our hypothetical negotiation, the two teams decide independently that they do not want to negotiate directly with each other. Each team knows that the opposing side is not prepared to give it what it wants. The neighborhood team knows that the company would never willingly agree to abandon the proposed project site and to leave the neighborhood in peace. The company team knows that the neighborhood would never willingly agree to allow the company to build a toxic-waste facility near the neighborhood.

Instead of pursuing fruitless negotiations with each other, the two opposing teams decide to negotiate with the regulatory agencies. From the neighborhood leaders' point of view, the regulatory agencies represent the best hope for keeping the toxic-waste facility away from the neighborhood. From the company leaders' point of view, the regulatory agencies represent the best hope for getting the project built at the chosen site. If the company is able to persuade the regulatory agencies to grant its permits, then the company will have the power of government and the weight of the law behind the project.

To conclude our example, let us roll the clock forward 8 months. Let's imagine what happens at the regulatory agencies' hearings.

Since the neighborhood team succeeded in persuading the agencies to hold the hearings in the community, turnout is not a problem. One thousand neighborhood people show up for the hearings, which are held in the local junior high school gymnasium. The neighborhood people not only come to the hearings, but they stay all day and most of the night.

All of the members of the media show up for the event. The toxic-waste site hearings are lead stories on the evening television news, on the larger radio stations' morning programs, and in the major daily newspapers the next day.

The elected officials turn out in force for the neighborhood team. They make very impressive, very persuasive speeches in opposition to the toxic-waste project. Particularly effective are the local state senators and state representatives, who inform the state regulatory agencies that they will be watching the agencies very closely to see what kind of decision they reach.

The neighborhood team's experts give powerful testimony in opposition to the facility. They cite the unproven nature of the technology involved. They also express concern regarding the strong potential for water contamination, and the certainty of air quality degradation, if the project is built.

The company is also well-prepared for the public hearings. Their lawyers and their experts have been softening up the regulators for months. Swarms of company personnel have been flooding the regulatory agencies with visits, with written information, and with videos. At the hearings, a dozen company lawyers and a dozen company technical experts make a compelling case for the safety of the proposed facility. Metall, the chief project engineer, cites his years of engineering experience and his months of work on the project. He publicly stakes his professional reputation on the safety of the project.

The leader of the company, Mr. Thicke, eloquently expresses his commitment to the well-being of the people in the neighborhood near the project. He lists the many charitable contributions his company has already made to worthwhile neighborhood programs. He tells the regulators and the crowd that he believes in good corporate citizenship. He promises that his company will always be a good neighbor to the people in the community.

Thicke states that 500 new jobs will be created by the toxic-waste facility. These will be high-paying jobs, and local people will be given preferential consideration in company hiring.

Thicke's presentation is followed by one from the president of the local chamber of commerce. The chamber president strongly supports the project. He states that it will provide tremendous economic benefits to the surrounding economically distressed area. The chamber of commerce president's speech is echoed by the president of the largest local bank.

The hearings adjourn after many hours of testimony. The regulators take the matter under advisement. They will make a decision within 6 months.

This concludes our hypothetical example. Which team do you think will win this environmental negotiation? The neighborhood team or the company team?

Step Five: React

"The real action is in the enemy's reaction."

Saul Alinsky

"The true rule, in determining to embrace, or to reject any thing, is not whether it has any evil in it; but whether it has more of evil than of good. There are few things *wholly* evil, or *wholly* good. Almost every thing, especially of govermental policy, is an inseparable compound of the two; so that our best judgement of the preponderance between them is continually demanded."

Abraham Lincoln, 1848

Your environmental negotiating team's action will generate some kind of reaction from your opponents, and it is the kind of reaction that your team creates that matters most of all. To quote from Saul Alinsky once again, "The real action is in the enemy's reaction." In other words, in practical terms it really doesn't matter all that much what you and your team did during the action phase. What really matters is the way your opponents reacted to what you did. You can be the greatest environmental negotiator in the world and have the most impressive team possible assembled on your behalf. Your strategy and timing can be perfect, but if all of your efforts fail to produce the desired reaction from your oppo-

157

nents, you haven't achieved what you wanted to achieve by negotiating.

A danger to guard against is the danger of being so impressed with yourself and with your team's performance that you forget to pay attention to the opposing team's reaction. It is entirely possible that you and your team could perform brilliantly, and you could still lose the ball game.

After you have played the big game, after you have engaged in the great contest of wills, gather your team leaders together and try to figure out who won. How did your opponents react to your action? Did you achieve your short-term goals and are you on your way to achieving your long-term goals? If you only achieved some of your goals, are you satisfied with what you did achieve or do you want to work for more?

There are an infinite number of possible reactions for the opposing team. I will list seven of the most common varieties, and I will offer you some suggestions regarding how your team should respond to these reactions. The seven most common reactions from the opposing team are the following:

1.   The hostile negative reaction
2.   The respectfully declining reaction
3.   The confused reaction
4.   The reluctant acceptance of some or all of your position
5.   The whole-hearted embrace of your position
6.   The compromise reaction
7.   The no-reaction-at-all reaction

The first reaction, the hostile negative reaction, is a frequent and easily understood response from the opposing side. You and your team do your best to persuade your opponents of the merit of your position, and they reply to you, "Not only no, but hell no!"

Your first thought is likely to be that this kind of reaction, the hostile negative reaction, is the worst sort of reaction you could get as an environmental negotiator. I assure you it is not. Certainly it would be a lot more pleasant if your opponents would respond to your proposals in a more favorable manner. It would be great if they just said yes to everything you wanted.

A nasty and complete rejection is not all negative, however. At least you know where you stand. That is not the case with several of the other more common types of reactions.

Furthermore, a mean and hostile reaction contains a lot of political energy. You can use that political energy against your opponent by performing some negotiating judo on him. You can cause your opponent to make a fool of himself by channeling his hostile reaction to your advantage.

A truly obnoxious adversary is a wonderful organizing tool for the environmental negotiator. You can use your opponent's behavior to motivate your team members onward to greater efforts, and you can enlist the sympathy and the support of previously neutral parties by highlighting the negative behavior of your opponent.

If your opponent reacts by attacking your team, rejoice. You can take the energy contained in his head-long assault on you, and you can turn it entirely to your advantage. It is rarely in your best interest to hide his attack on you under a bushel basket. Rather, it is preferable to let the full light of day shine on your opponent's reaction. Tell everybody in town about the terrible things that your opponent did to you and said to you. Your opponent's hot reaction will help you to heat things up nicely.

The second possible reaction, the respectful declination, on the other hand, tends to take the energy out of your organization. This reaction is defined as being the polite, friendly rejection of everything you hope to achieve through your negotiation. The hostile negative reaction makes your players angry, and if you play your cards right, it motivates them to do more. The friendly, respectfully declining reaction tends to make you and your team members feel guilty for having asked your opponent for anything. What your opponent is attempting to say with this kind of reaction is, " I will like you. I would love to help you reach your goals, but I cannot."

One of the most common forms of respectfully declining is for your opponent to say to you, "I would love to help you with this issue, but it's not an issue that we handle in my department. Why don't you go talk with someone in this other department over there?"

If your opponent respectfully declines by referring you to someone else, you should respond by researching immediately whether or not the opponent who respectfully declines has the power to give you what you want. It is possible that you and your team members performed faulty research, that you are talking to the wrong person in the wrong shop.

If you have performed all the strategic steps I have told you to perform, however, it is seriously unlikely that you and your team are in the wrong place talking to the wrong person. What is far more likely is the fact that your opponent does have the power to give you what you want, that you are talking to the right person, and that your opponent is telling you no in a very sneaky way.

Don't let your opponent get away with it. Don't let him convince you and your players that he cannot help you, even though he wants to help you. Make it clear to him and to your players that you know that he has the power to meet your goals. Be very direct with him and say that you know he does have the power to give you what you want, but that he is choosing not to be helpful for reasons that you do not understand.

Hopefully your opponent will respond by telling you specifically those constraints that bind his hands, or by explaining to you concretely what steps you could take to loosen those constraints. He may not have all the power he appears to have or, in theory, he should have.

Alternatively, your opponent may respond by admitting to you that he could help you, but that he is choosing not to do so. You are getting somewhere in your negotiation if you can get your adversary to tell you exactly what it is about your proposal that he finds objectionable. If you know what your opponent's objections are, you can address them. If you do not know what your opponent's objections are, it is considerably more difficult.

A third way the respectful decliner may respond to your challenge is to become angry at you for pushing him and for insulting his integrity. If he becomes angry at you, his reaction will change from respectfully declining to hostile and negative. I have already told you what to do if your opponent reacts in a hostile, negative manner.

A totally different reaction that you may experience is the confused reaction. With this reaction your opponent gives you and your team a blank stare and he says, "I don't understand. I don't see what the problem is." Or he might say, "What are you talking about? I don't understand a word you are saying." Or he might stare out into space and say nothing at all except for an occasional sigh or grunt.

As a negotiator, you have to decide whether your opponent is truly confused or whether he is engaging in strategic ignorance. If he is genuinely confused, you need to restate your position patiently and carefully, using language and metaphors that are common to all human experience. If you have explained your position to him in this manner, and he still seems confused, he is either seriously incompetent or he is trying to fool you.

You will be there at the negotiation. I, most likely, won't be. You will have to decide whether your opponent is hopelessly incompetent or whether he is trying to fool you by acting confused. If you conclude that he is incapable of understanding you and your issues, then get away from him as fast as you can. It is useless to negotiate with him any further. If you conclude that he is fooling around with you, tell him so. You don't have to be aggressive about it. Just make it clear to him in a cheerful way that you know he is playing around with you and that you expect better from him. If you correctly guess that he really knows what you are saying, but that he is merely playing games with you, he will be pleased and impressed that you have found him out. It is flattering for you to realize that he is not really the fool he would like to appear to be.

The reluctant acceptance of some or all of your position is another possible reaction, and it is an encouraging reaction at that. It is a terrific feeling to have your wishes granted, even if those wishes are granted partially or grudgingly.

If your goals are partially met by your opponent, you have to huddle with your team members and decide if that is sufficient for you. If your opponent's partial agreement is not satisfactory, then you have to go back and negotiate for more.

If the partial agreement is satisfactory or if your opponent reluctantly gives you everything you ask for in your negotiation, you and your team members need to switch gears and ask yourselves another question. That question is, does this opponent really intend to give us all of the things he is grudgingly agreeing to give, or is he lying to get us out of his hair? In other words, is your opponent sincerely going to follow through on his commitments or is he engaged in calculated lying?

You should be especially suspicious of someone who grudgingly agrees to some or all of your proposals, but who appears to get nothing in return for himself out of the deal. A hostile acceptance can be more dangerous than an outright rejection. Your negotiating opponent does not have to like every aspect of the negotiated settlement, but it is important for him to feel comfortable with the settlement. It is critical that your opponent believes he has benefitted in some way from the negotiation. Otherwise, he will be looking for every opportunity to break the commitments he so reluctantly agreed to.

The remedy for the grudging acceptance reaction is to offer your opponent something that he wants that you do not mind giving up. You can expand your agreement with him to include things that you know are important to him, but that do no violence to your goals. By doing this, by expanding the agreement, you are giving your opponent greater dignity. You are also giving your opponent a sense of ownership regarding your agreement. If your opponent feels a sense of dignity and if your opponent feels a sense of ownership, he will keep his commitments to you in a much more reliable fashion.

A fifth possible reaction is the whole-hearted embrace of your position. This type of reaction is rare, unnerving, and exhilarating. It almost never happens in environmental negotiations.

If your opponent tells you that he agrees with all of your positions and that he is enthusiastically willing to commit to accomplishing them, my advice to you is to take a deep breath and to step back from your opponent for a moment. It may be rude, but now is the appropriate time to look the gift horse in the mouth. First, repeat your positions slowly and simply to make certain that your opponent understood them. Make certain that your opponent is agreeing not only to the goals you have presented, but also that he is agreeing to take the concrete steps that are necessary to accomplish those goals. Finally, try to get your opponent to tell you why it is in his self-interest to embrace your position so whole-heartedly. If your opponent can convincingly explain his complete acceptance in terms of his own self-interest, then you should probably believe that his whole-hearted embrace is sincere.

If he cannot explain his agreement in terms of his own self-interest, or if he tries to tell you that he is agreeing with you because he is such a nice guy, reach quickly for your wallet to make certain it is secure. You may have found an opponent who is cheerfully willing to give you everything you ask for, someone who is so generous he will give you what you want without any regard for what he wants. You may also find some day a person who will gladly give you his winning lottery ticket without expecting anything in return. Both of these things are possible, but you would be wise not to count on them.

The more likely reaction, and the more reliable reaction, is the compromise reaction. With this reaction your opponent is telling you that you can have part of what you want, provided you are willing to give him part of what he wants. In the compromise reaction, your opponent's self-interest is usually obvious. He is being frank about it. He is trying to see that his needs are met, but he is also attempting to accommodate your needs.

The compromise reaction requires an active response from you. You and your team have to go to work immediately. You must carefully scrutinize your opponent's compromise proposal to determine if it is acceptable to you and to your team members.

You have many questions to ask yourselves. Does the compromise proposal address your team's priority goals? Are your opponent's demands reasonable and are those demands compatible with your goals? If your team does not find your opponent's compromise proposal acceptable, can you think of a counter-offer that would be acceptable to you and to your opponent? If you and your opponent are able to find a mutually acceptable compromise, what methods will you and your opponent use to make certain that both sides keep their agreement?

The compromise reaction on your opponent's part raises many questions that need to be answered on your part. The compromise reaction requires hard work and considerable effort as well. The questions that this type of reaction raises are fundamentally healthy ones, however, and the effort that this reaction requires you to expend is usually effort well-spent.

The willingness to compromise is one of the most constructive responses you can receive from the opposing side during an environmental negotiation. In the long run, it is generally a more honest response and a more reliable one than the other types of reactions that appear to be more favorable.

The final reaction I want to discuss is the no-reaction-at-all reaction. Every environmental negotiator encounters this type of reaction from time to time. You state your goals, and your opponent yawns. You take action against your opponent, and he ignores you. You offer to compromise, and your opponent stares out into space. The no-reaction-at-all reaction is an extremely frustrating reaction.

This reaction is usually caused by one of two things. First, it could be caused by your opponent's belief that it is to his strategic advantage not to react to you. Secondly, it could be caused by the fact that your opponent does not know how to negotiate, i.e., he is an incompetent negotiator. You must try to determine which of these two reasons applies to your specific negotiator.

If your opponent believes it is in his best interest not to resist you, if his failure to respond is a strategic decision on his part, your response must be to persuade him that that is not the case. You must convince him through your words and deeds that he has seriously miscalculated regarding his best interest. You and your team members have to take actions, sometimes dramatic actions, to convince your opponent that he is better off responding to you. Your team has to make it too expensive for your opponent to continue ignoring you. This practice is referred to in the political trade as "turning up the heat." It is a time-honored practice, and I heartily endorse it if your opponent is purposely ignoring your actions.

On the other hand, I recommend a different approach if your opponent is not reacting to you because he is an incompetent negotiator. If your opponent does not know how to negotiate, it will do you no good to pound him senseless for that shortcoming. What you have to do instead is to assume the responsibility of negotiating for both sides. Strange as it may sound, you have to imagine your opponent's response to your actions and you have to state that response for him if he is unable to say it for himself. You debate both sides of the issue in front of your opponent. You make a compromise offer, and you give him a possible counter-offer.

By conducting this kind of debate with yourself in front of your opponent, you are helping him to hold up his side of the negotiation. You would think your opponent would be insulted and resentful of your attempt to speak for both sides of the negotiation. If your opponent is a competent negotiator, he will be insulted and resentful because he is perfectly capable of speaking for himself. If your opponent is not a skilled and experienced negotiator, however, he will genuinely appreciate your efforts to help him out under most circumstances. Your negotiating for both sides should not be done in an obvious way or in a way that is demeaning to your opponent. If you do it subtly and sensitively, you will be astounded at how far you can move the negotiation along. Your incompetent opponent may not react at all to your proposals at first, but he will react very favorably in the end to your technique of negotiating for both sides.

Seven Negative Emotional Reactions and How to Help Your Team Deal With Them

Negotiating actions on your team's part can cause a variety of reactions on the part of the opposing team. I have just summarized the seven most common reactions you will receive from the opposing team, and I have suggested several appropriate strategies for dealing with those reactions. Keep in mind, however, that the opposing team's response to your actions can also cause your team members to experience several types of emotional reactions, some of them negative.

As an environmental negotiator, you cannot assume responsibility for the emotional behavior of the opposing team. You must, however, assume responsibility for handling the negative emotional reactions of your team members.

I will list seven negative emotional reactions that are experienced at one time or another by every environmental negotiating team. Then I will suggest how you change those negative emotions and redirect your team members into more productive directions.

The seven negative emotional reactions that your team members can experience as a result of the opposing team's behavior are as follows:

1. Anger
2. Frustration
3. Embarrassment
4. Feelings of inadequacy
5. Defeat
6. Fatigue
7. Boredom

When you see your team members exhibiting these negative emotions, the first thing you should do is to honestly acknowledge to them that they have those feelings. It is phony and it is counter-productive to pretend that everything is all right when it clearly is not. You can add that it is perfectly normal and OK to have negative feelings about the negotiation. Tell your team members that you feel the same way that they do or that you have, in the past, felt the same way.

Once you have acknowledged your team members' feelings, once you have told them that their feelings are natural and that you share their feelings, you should begin to move to change those negative emotions into more positive ones. There is no shame in having bad feelings about the progress of an environmental negotiation. The shame is in allowing bad feelings to stagnate and to fester, thereby crippling the effectiveness of your negotiating team.

Let me start with the emotion of anger. Bottled up inside an individual or expressed by a team player against his own team, anger can be deadly and destructive. Dissention in the ranks can kill any organization or any team. While it is possible that your team members are really angry at each other, it is more likely that they are angry at the players on the opposing team and that they are upset about the tactics being utilized by the opposing team.

As I have said previously in this book, anger is a form of human energy. Anger can destroy your team if it is directed inward, or it can motivate and inspire your team if it is directed outward at the opposing team. Your job as an environmental negotiator is to take your team members' anger and to direct it outward at the oppos-ing side. Your task is to take the tremendous human energy contained in your team members' anger and to use it to accomplish the negotiating work at hand. The best thing you can do for an angry team member is to give him a lot of work, work that is clearly aimed at inflicting damage on the opposing team's strength and credibility.

The same applies if the team members' anger is directed at you, the team leader. Remind them that you are not the enemy. Take the anger that is directed at you and channel it outward toward the opposition. Give them work to do that puts their anger to good use.

The second negative emotion I listed, frustration, is a particular form of anger. In environmental negotiations, frustration is usu-ally anger over the slow rate of progress of the negotiations. If your team members are showing signs of frustration, you need to pull out the timetable that you established and see how you are doing as a team in adhering to that timetable. If you and your team are right on schedule, pointing that fact out to them will dissipate much of their frustration. If checking your timetable reveals that you are, indeed, behind schedule, you should use that discovery to challenge you team members to get back on schedule. If they are truly progressing too slowly, you have to motivate them to do what it takes to make faster progress. Point out to them that sitting around feeling frustrated at the lack of progress will not help the situation. Review the steps that you and your team members agreed to take to realize your team goals. See where you have bogged down, and get to work to correct it. Use your team goals to inspire your players to greater effort.

Embarrassment is another common negative emotion that you or your team members may experience during the course of a negotiation. Humor, particularly self-deprecating humor, is the antidote for embarrassment. Everyone makes embarrassing mistakes. Everyone finds himself in embarrassing situations. Reassure your teammates when they are embarrassed by telling them humorous war stories from your past. Make sure that, in choosing your story, the joke is on you and not on your team members. It is a high risk move, an unnecessarily dangerous move, to make light of a team member at a time when he is already self-conscious and sensitive.

Feelings of embarrassment are generally temporary nuisances that you can easily correct. Feelings of inadequacy, on the other hand, are far more serious and far more potentially devastating to your team. Embarrassment can usually be handled with a few clever comments and a couple of war stories. Feelings of inadequacy are not so easily dismissed.

When your team members tell you that they feel inadequate, when they say that they are not up to the demands of the negotiation, what they are telling you is that, in their heart of hearts, they believe they are incompetent environmental negotiators. They will tell you that they are not smart enough or aggressive enough or educated enough or good-looking enough to succeed at environmental negotiations. They believe that they are losers, and they will try to convince you that they are losers.

If these feelings of inadequacy are allowed to persist, there is no way your team can succeed at environmental negotiations. Your team will never win if it is convinced it cannot win.

Do not ignore feelings of inadequacy on the part of your team players. Do not kid yourself that feelings of inadequacy on the part of your players will not affect the performance of your team.

You must correct your team's feelings of inadequacy through confidence-building measures that strike at the heart of their insecurities. For example, if your team members feel inadequate because they do not have a scientific or technical background, correct those feelings by giving them a crash course in science and technology that is applicable to your particular environmental negotiation. Bring in a scientist or engineer to explain things to your players.

Make certain that you choose a scientist/translator or an engineer/translator to educate your team. If you select your average jargon-speaking, superior-acting scientist or engineer, your team members will come away from the experience feeling more inadequate than they felt before.

If your team members believe they are inadequate because they are not sufficiently aggressive, give them some mildly assertive, mildly aggressive tasks. Select tasks at which they are very likely to succeed. As they perform these initial tasks successfully, gradually increase the degree of difficulty of the tasks that they must perform. Give them actions to take that incrementally increase the needs for assertiveness and the need for aggressiveness.

If you structure your negotiation to guarantee that your players experience early success, they will begin to stop thinking of themselves as losers. When they stop thinking of themselves as losers, the feelings of inadequacy will disappear.

When your players feel inadequate, they are so afraid of failing that they do not want to try to win. But what if your players really try? What if they give it their best shot and still lose?

Feelings of defeat are an inevitable part of environmental negotiations. Those who have never lost have never played the game for any length of time. How do you and your teammates bounce back from a tough defeat?

The first step in the healing process is to sit down together and to analyze why you lost. It is not particularly pretty or in itself uplifting to go over your failed negotiation to find out what went wrong. It is a necessary part of cleansing yourselves of your defeat, however. Studying your mistakes is also a useful way to avoid repeating them.

Once you have figured out where you went wrong and why your team lost, it is a good idea to begin immediately preparing for a future environmental negotiation. Start the process over. Go back to step one, research, and start working your way through the five steps I have given you:

1. Do research
2. Take stock
3. Organize
4. Act
5. React

Do not allow your team members or yourself to wallow in feelings of defeat. Action is the best cure for feeling defeated.

As you work through the five steps again, pay close attention to the new goals you are setting and to the timetable you are establishing. You and your team may have failed because you attempted to accomplish too much too soon. You might have to scale back your expectations and to extend your timetable.

Another negative feeling that is especially common in lengthy environmental negotiations is fatigue. By fatigue I mean the mental tiredness that you and your team may experience, not physical weariness or the need for a good night's rest.

If a negotiation drags on and on, you and your teammates may become sick of it. If you are trying to solve the problem of water pollution in a nearby lake, for example, you could be seeing so many fecal coliform counts that you want to scream if you see another one. You may become thoroughly disgusted with the parties on the other side of the table with whom you are attempting to negotiate.

The antidote for fatigue in environmental negotiations is simple and straightforward. Get away from the negotiation for awhile. Drop it and do something else until you feel your old enthusiasm for the subject come creeping back.

It is rarely a good idea to continue a negotiation after you have become sick and tired of it. Back off, get away from it, and come back refreshed another day.

Fatigue comes from doing too much of the same thing. Boredom is the result of doing too little of anything.

Your team will become fatigued if it does too much of the same thing for too long. Your team will become painfully bored if it does too little of anything for too long.

Remember Saul Alinsky's statement, "Organizations need action as an individual needs oxygen." If your players are acting bored, they are trying to tell you something: "Give us something challenging to do!" If your team as a whole is not bored, but individual players on your team are, those individual players are begging you for more work to do. Satisfy their needs by giving them bigger and more serious assignments for your negotiation.

PART IV:

TACTICS

AN INTRODUCTION TO TACTICS

"We will either find a way or make one."

Hannibal

"I will not only give 'em battle, I will lick 'em"

Dick Dowling, 1863

Having progressed to this point in the book, you now have the basic understanding necessary to be an effective environmental negotiator. You know the players of the game, and you know the different varieties of environmental negotiation. You know how the rules of the game change depending on which variety of the game you are playing. You understand the five steps in the environmental negotiating process, and you have the clear strategic sense to accomplish those five steps in an orderly fashion. You know how to set realistic and inspiring goals, and you know that you must have a timetable for achieving those goals.

What you need now are some practical nuts-and-bolts techniques for achieving your goals. You need some tried-and-true tactical approaches that you can use to accomplish your goals.

I will give you nine effective tactical approaches that I have

173

experienced during my years as an environmental negotiator. All of them are useful at one time or another.

Your job as an environmental negotiator is to pick from this bag of tricks the style that correctly matches you, your team, and the circumstances of your negotiation. You also want to select the style that will have the maximum positive effect on the opposing team. The negotiating style you select must fit the specific environmental negotiation you are conducting.

There are, of course, more than nine styles of environmental negotiation. The list of styles that you can successfully utilize is endless.

Use your personal experience and your individual creativity to create new styles that are uniquely suited to you. Experiment and see what works. If you discover a new approach that is particularly useful, please let me know about it.

The Nine Styles of Environmental Negotiation

These are the nine common styles of environmental negotiation. Each of these approaches either works or does not work, depending on you, your team, the opposition, and the circumstances of your negotiation. These techniques have been used by me effectively, and they have been used against me effectively. Learn each one of them, for you will certainly experience all of them during your work as an environmental negotiator.

The nine common styles of environmental negotiation are as follows:

1. The blacksmith approach
2. The surgical strike
3. The "know-it-all expert" approach
4. The warm, friendly approach
5. The "bore-them-to-death" approach
6. The arrogant, obnoxious S.O.B. technique
7. The "come-let-us-reason-together" preacher
8. The kamikaze pilot
9. The "not-negotiating-at-all" negotiation

I will describe each of these styles separately, and I will suggest the correct circumstances for using each of them. I will give you examples of each technique in actual use. I will suggest ways you can successfully resist each one of these approaches if your opponent tries to use one or more of them against you.

THE BLACKSMITH APPROACH

"If the facts are with you, pound on the facts.
If the law is with you, pound on the law.
If the facts aren't with you and the law is not with you, pound on the table."

An old lawyer's advice to a new lawyer

In legal circles, the above quote is passed down from one generation of lawyers to the next. I have no idea who said it first, so I offer it to you as an old lawyer's advice to a new lawyer.

This particular quote, a favorite of mine, is a fine introduction to the negotiating style called the blacksmith approach because it emphasizes the word *pound*. If you choose the blacksmith approach, that is what you will do for the duration of the negotiation. You will pound away on the opposition until it becomes malleable.

Before I practiced the art of environmental negotiation, I thought that environmental negotiations were rather subtle affairs, something akin to, for example, the fine tuning of electronic stereo equipment. I imagined that I would be like a skilled electronic technician. With a precise, delicate touch, I would adjust public policies and change environmental practices to make things right.

After practicing environmental negotiations for the past 10 years, I have become convinced that there is little subtlety in most environmental negotiations. Far from resembling the tuning of electronic stereo equipment, I have discovered that most of my work as a negotiator is like that of the old-fashioned blacksmith.

In order to shape cold, unyielding iron, I build a big fire and I stoke it white hot with powerful bellows. I stick the iron in the fire, and I continue to squeeze down on my bellows. I make the fire as hot as possible. Gradually the metal in the fire begins to soften. When the metal is softened, I grab the biggest pair of tongs and the biggest hammer I can handle. I take the piece of softened metal and I pound away on it until it takes the shape I want it to take.

The blacksmith approach is the classic technique used in informal public negotiations. In the informal public negotiation, neither side is willing to negotiate with the other side. In fact, most of the time during informal public negotiations, the opposing sides are not even willing to talk directly to one another. Under these circumstances, the two opposing teams use the media to negotiate indirectly with each other. Reporters shuttle back and forth between the two hostile camps. They gather information and they discover the positions of one side, and they dutifully report that information and those positions to the other side. The two sides pound away on each other using the media as their instrument.

In my experience, the blacksmith approach is the most common style of environmental negotiation. What it lacks in subtlety, it more than makes up for in terms of brute force and effectiveness. The blacksmith approach is not pretty to watch, but it works. The blacksmith approach is the technique you should consider using whenever you come up against someone who is unwilling to negotiate with you. This approach is most pleasurable if you use it against a large, powerful, uncaring, unyielding opponent.

Your opponent, for example, might be a politically popular mayor who doesn't want to stop local businesses from polluting the air in your city. You politely ask the mayor to enter into environmental negotiations with you and your team, but he refuses to do so. Not only is he unwilling to talk, he is also unwilling to act in any meaningful way to clean up the air. It may be time for you and your team to try the blacksmith approach.

Soften up the mayor by staging large-scale, public relations assaults on him. Show up at the city council public hearing with 100 parents of asthmatic children, and blame the mayor, by name, for the devastating health affects of poor air quality in your city. Write scores of letters to your newspapers complaining about the evils of dirty air and about the mayor's failure to do anything about it. Conduct a media blitz. Schedule interviews with sympathetic reporters. Appear on radio and on TV talkshows to complain about the city's air quality problems and about the mayor. Enlist the help of sympathetic councilmembers, and especially those who might want to run for the mayor's job. Get them to pound away on the mayor with you. Get them to join you in blaming the mayor for poor air quality.

As I have said, there is little subtlety in this approach. No one is fooling anyone. The mayor will know exactly what you are doing, and he will know exactly why you are doing it. He will resent like hell the fact that you and your team are banging away on him day after day.

If he is worth anything as a politician, however, he will begin to soften his position if you and your team do your jobs effectively. He will probably not agree to negotiate directly with you on the issue, but if you and your team members have applied enough heat to him, he will begin to change his position on your issue.

Once he has softened in his resistance to your position, grab a big hammer and a big pair of tongs. Get ahold of the mayor and don't let go. Continue to publicly pound away on him. Tell him through the media the specific steps he needs to take to clean up the air. When he protests the rough treatment, ignore him. Let him howl. Pound away, without mercy and without regret, until the mayor gives you the clean air you want.

The blacksmith approach is an endurance contest. If you and your team can keep the heat at a high level, if you pound away as the opposition begins to soften, then you will succeed in getting what you want out of your environmental negotiation.

Blast away at every opportunity. Do not worry about being too obvious or about offending the opposing team. If the opposing team was being flexible and cooperative, you and your team would not have used the blacksmith approach. Your aim in using the blacksmith approach is to shape the opposition's behavior in order to realize your negotiating goals. If the opposing team decides, after much heat and pounding, to meet your demands, it doesn't matter if the opposing team likes you or your tactics. You have achieved your goals. You did it by using the blacksmith approach, and you probably could not have done it any other way.

THE SURGICAL STRIKE

"... a skillfully performed surgical procedure, carried out efficiently and gently, with dispatch and minimal blood loss is still most likely to ensure low morbidity and mortality"

Denton A. Cooley, M.D.
Reflections and Observations: Essays of Denton A. Cooley

The surgical strike is the complete opposite of the blacksmith approach. With the surgical strike, subtlety and timing are everything. Subtlety, timing, and the swift application of overwhelming force are the essential characteristics of the surgical strike. A surgical strike is the precise application of overpowering force to a carefully selected, sympathetic target in order to achieve your negotiating goals.

It is best suited for negotiations in which your opponent is predisposed to give you what you want, provided he can do it without too much noise and fuss. Imagine that your particular negotiation is like a pair of evenly balanced scales, and that the outcome hangs delicately in the balance. The surgical strike is the perfect tool to use to tip the scales, and the outcome of the negotiation, in your favor.

Let me describe an instance in which I used the surgical strike to good effect. As a city councilmember, I had been working with environmental groups for some time to beef up the environmental enforcement programs in the city's health department. Despite our best efforts, we had achieved no dramatic progress in gaining the additional departmental funding that would be required to implement strengthened environmental enforcement programs. The price tag for the program improvements was approximately $500,000.

Through our research, we had discovered that the new annual budget was about to be released with no new money allocated for improved environmental enforcement. We also had discovered that the chief financial officer, the person who was drafting the budget, was a closet environmentalist who was sympathetic to our position. We, furthermore, found out he hated public conflicts and public controversies, especially if those conflicts and controversies were related in any way to his beloved budget document.

Given this set of circumstances, my team and I decided to use the surgical strike. We quietly assembled the leaders of the largest and most reputable environmental organizations in town. We developed a specific budget proposal for increased environmental enforcement. We practiced our presentation with each other before we scheduled an appointment to see the chief financial officer of the city. When we were certain that we were ready as a negotiating team, we then requested a private, friendly meeting with the chief financial officer in his City Hall office. We said nothing at all to the press about our proposal or about our upcoming meeting.

At the meeting itself, we introduced ourselves to the chief financial officer, we identified the organizations we were representing, and we pointed out specifically how many members each organization had. The total number of members represented by the environmental leaders present was truly impressive. The 10 leaders at the meeting were speaking for over 10,000 citizens of our city.

We handed the chief financial officer a written copy of our budget proposal, and then we took turns carefully explaining the significance of each line item in it. He asked us several questions, and we answered them to his satisfaction.

He was clearly leaning our way, but he needed a little additional nudge. We pointed out to him that we had chosen to come to him quietly and privately because we had great confidence in his interest in our cause. We told him that we knew he did not like a lot of controversy surrounding his budget, that he preferred to solve budget problems before his budgets were submitted to city council. We concluded by saying that we did not plan to tell the press about our concerns or about our meeting with him, if our proposal was included in his upcoming budget. We told him we would rather handle our business with him quietly and privately, that we would hate to have to publicly pound away on him and the mayor for failing to provide proper funding levels for environmental enforcement programs.

The chief financial officer praised us for our constructive approach, and he agreed to put all of our proposals in the upcoming budget. The surgical strike had worked. We knew it had worked when we found our entire proposal had been incorporated into the annual city budget that he released a few weeks after our private meeting.

The "Know-It-All Expert" Approach

> "The good Expert needs to be street smart and possess a strong theoretical background. Street smartness is just plain essential, since lawsuits generally arise from practical difficulties. The credentials of a good Expert should at least match those of the opposing Expert. In the battle of the Experts, you do not want to be outgunned by a resume that looks like the Manhattan phone directory. A good Expert acts and looks dignified, dresses in good taste, and has a confident demeanor and attitude. A good Expert is exactly that—*the* Expert in the field."
>
> Jack V. Matson

The "know-it-all expert" approach is the favorite tactic of scientists and of engineers, although I have also seen bluffing nonprofessionals use this tactic and get away with it. If you and your negotiating team have access to engineers or to scientists with strong environmental credentials, you can use this approach to intimidate the opposing team and to roll over them intellectually.

Here is how you use the "know-it-all expert" approach. A scientist or an engineer from your negotiating team proclaims that he is an expert on the subject being negotiated, say, wastewater

185

treatment plant design. He points out that he has an undergraduate engineering degree and a master's degree in civil engineering. He states that he has designed wastewater treatment plants for 25 years and that he has taught the subject of wastewater plant design at the local university for the past 12 years. He recites a long and impressive list of the many clients who have used his wastewater plant design services over the years.

Once your engineer or scientist has established himself as the most knowledgeable person present at the negotiation, he proceeds to define the environmental problem that is being negotiated. He gives his solution to the problem, and he proclaims that it is the only professionally correct solution to that problem. The solution that your expert presents is the solution you and your team have agreed upon well in advance of the actual negotiation. Although you and your team are well aware of the fact that there are other viable solutions, your expert presents your solution as though it were the only reasonable one possible.

Once your expert has presented your team's solution, he busies himself refuting any challenges to that solution. He ridicules the other team's proposals. He claims that the people presenting other options do not understand the facts. He says that those who differ with him are unreasonable and are not sufficiently educated on the subject to make intelligent comments.

The "know-it-all expert" does not need to become belligerent with the opposing team members. He, instead, takes on the air of being above the fray. He has truth and wisdom; others do not. He acts secure in the knowledge that he is correct and that his opponents are perhaps well-meaning, but totally misinformed.

I know an engineer in my city who is the master of the "know-it-all expert" approach. I will call him Perry Sage. A few years ago, Perry Sage came to testify before a city council committee that was charged with preparing a master water plan for our city. He was advocating the construction of a new reservoir on the western side of the city.

When Perry's turn to testify arrived, he began by reciting his resume. He had undergraduate and graduate degrees in engineering. He had an impressive list of satisfied customers. He had extensive experience in designing water supply projects. Clearly, he was an expert on the subject.

Then he offered his solution to our water supply problem: the construction of a western reservoir. He said that it was the only reasonable, cost-effective solution to our problem. He smiled and shook his head when a committee member asked him about an alternative eastern reservoir proposal. It made no sense, Perry told us. The eastern reservoir idea was not a viable option. The only viable option for the city was the construction of a western reservoir.

When Perry was pressed for more details, he immediately produced detailed plans, maps, and data that he happened to bring along. When committee members wanted to debate him, he would refer them back to his plans or his maps or his numbers for an explanation.

Perry would have persuaded the committee to adopt his plan right then and there, except for one thing. The Public Works Department director had anticipated Perry Sage's tactical approach. The director had the foresight to bring along his own expert on water supply. The director's expert brought along another set of maps, plans, and numbers. The director's expert pointed out that by building the eastern reservoir the city would realize much more water for the same expenditure of money than it would realize by building a western reservoir.

I have watched scientists and engineers shatter the opposing team by using the "know-it-all expert" tactic. It is a tactic that works especially well if the opposing team is composed of people who do not have much in the way of scientific training, and if the opposing team members do not have a great deal of confidence in their own native intelligence.

It is a tactic that does not work well, in fact, it is a tactic that does not work at all, if the opposing team is loaded with players who have scientific training and who understand how this tactic is used. You can counter this tactic successfully by simply maintaining confidence in your own intellectual abilities or by presenting your own "know-it-all expert" to counter theirs.

The "know-it-all expert" approach is, in reality, a tactical bluff. It works every time if you are going up against opposing players who are easily bluffed. It doesn't work at all if the opposing team members understand your tactic and refuse to be intimidated by it.

THE WARM, FRIENDLY
APPROACH

"You can catch more flies with honey than with vinegar."

Southern folk expression

The warm, friendly approach is the tactical style preferred by two very diverse groups of people: sincere, honest people and lobbyists. This approach is based on persuading the opposing team that you are their friend, that you only want what is in their interest. The person using this approach will tell you the following: He only wants what is best for you. He only wants what you want.

As he negotiates with you, he minimizes the differences between your team's position and his team's position. He will try to persuade you that your team's position and his team's position are exactly the same, except for a few technical details that are unimportant. Since he is your friend, since his position on the issue at hand is the same as yours, and since he only wants what is best for you, there is no harm in adopting his negotiating position as your own. Right? Maybe.

The person using the warm, friendly approach may be a genu-

189

ine friend of yours, or he may be a lobbyist. The warm, friendly approach is the tactical style preferred by most lobbyists. This tactical approach could be an act of friendship or it could be an act of seduction. The challenge to you as an environmental negotiator is to determine which it is.

The warm, friendly approach as the lobbyist uses it is an exercise in the art of seduction. The lobbyist is not your friend; his position in the negotiation is not the same as yours, and he could care less about what is best for you. His warm, friendly approach is a technique that he has used time and time again to entrap unsuspecting, unsophisticated, would-be environmental negotiators.

The best way to understand the warm, friendly approach as it is practiced by a lobbyist is to permit a skilled one to give you the treatment. Watch carefully how he works on you. He exudes warmth and charm. He repeats over and over again how impressed he is with your intelligence, your good looks, your outstanding personality, your beliefs, and your values. He tells you all the reasons why you are special. He points out why you are wiser than your other team members. You are more reasonable, more flexible. You have a better understanding of the issue, you are more responsible than the others in your group.

He stresses that he is your friend, and because he is your friend, he only wants what is best for you. Besides, you and he want the same things. You are both after the same goals, he tells you. There is no reason why you cannot adopt his position and still feel good about yourself.

Once you have experienced this kind of warm, friendly approach, you are well-prepared to perform it on others. Believe me, it works much of the time. Countless people will roll over for you. They will embrace your position as their own because you have told them that you are their friend and because you have told them that your position is the same as theirs.

I frequently use the warm, friendly approach in my environmental negotiations. I am, of course, a painfully sincere person. I would never attempt to deceive another by using this technique. Well, perhaps, I should give you an example of a time I used this approach so you can make up your own mind whether I was being a friendly guy or whether I was acting like a lobbyist.

Our regional Subsidence Board is an important regulatory body that is responsible for controlling subsidence, the sinking of the ground in relationship to sea level. Subsidence occurs when excessive amounts of underground water are pumped out. Subsidence was proceeding at an alarming rate in the western part of our city, and the Subsidence Board was doing nothing to stop it. The Subsidence Board at the time was composed of entirely white males who were not especially sensitive to environmental concerns.

My friends in the environmental community and I concluded that we had to get more environmentally conscious people on the Subsidence Board before we would make any progress in controlling subsidence. We scheduled a private meeting with the mayor to discuss her appointments to the Subsidence Board. The meeting took place in her office.

The tone of the meeting was decidedly warm and friendly, even though the mayor was not particularly sensitive to environmental issues. A couple of environmental leaders and I told the mayor that we knew she shared our concerns about the rapid rate of subsidence in the western part of our city. We agreed with her that the Subsidence Board was the appropriate agency for addressing the problem. We said that we supported her commitment to appointing more women and more minorities to boards and commissions.

After she reaffirmed her commitment to appointing more women and more minorities to boards and commissions, my friends and I presented two resumes to the mayor for her consideration in filling two upcoming vacancies on the Subsidence Board. One of the resumes belonged to a black man who was an experienced corporate engineer; the other belonged to a white female who was an engineer for Exxon. The mayor was pleased with the resumes, and later on with the two people themselves. She appointed both of them to the Subsidence Board.

What we forgot to tell the mayor in our warm, friendly negotiation with her was the fact that both of these individuals were committed environmentalists who were determined to address the problem of subsidence. They shook up the Subsidence Board more than the mayor or anyone else anticipated. The board began to take steps to control subsidence.

The warm, friendly approach works on a large percentage of humanity, especially with opponents who are basically sincere, caring people. There is one group of humanity that the warm, friendly approach does not work on, however. The warm, friendly approach does not work on professional lobbyists. They will laugh out loud if you repeat their own lines back to them. If you exude warmth and charm by the boatload, if you tell a lobbyist that you are his friend and that you only want what is best for him, he will get a case of the giggles that resembles convulsions. He will laugh for 5 minutes without ceasing.

Once he is able to contain himself, he will get a somber expression on his face. He will look you straight in the eye and he will say, "What are you trying to pull on me? You should never try to kid a kidder."

The best way to resist the warm, friendly approach is to be warmer and friendlier than your opponents. If your negotiating opponents are sincerely your friends, they will appreciate you for being so nice to them. If the people using this approach on you are not your friends, then you will drive then crazy by being so warm and so friendly towards them.

THE ARROGANT, OBNOXIOUS, S.O.B. APPROACH

> "If the enemy general is obstinate and prone to anger, insult and enrage him, so that he will be irritated and confused, and without a plan will reckessly advance against you."
>
> Sun Tzu
> *The Art of War*

The arrogant, obnoxious, S.O.B. approach is, in appearance, the complete opposite of the warm, friendly approach. The warm, friendly approach is based on stroking your opponent's ego and on building up his self-esteem. The arrogant, obnoxious, S.O.B. approach is based on attacking your opponent's ego and on breaking down his self-esteem.

The arrogant, obnoxious, S.O.B. approach is a favorite of lawyers, although I have also seen it used by industrialists, developers and more than a few environmental activists. The purpose of the S.O.B. approach is to destroy the opposing team's will to fight. The arrogant, obnoxious S.O.B. makes the negotiating experience so unpleasant that the opposing team is often willing to agree to anything in order for the ordeal to end.

A lawyer I know, I will call him Bob "The Tiger" Thompson, is a master of the arrogant, obnoxious, S.O.B. approach. He begins his environmental negotiation by immediately attacking the opposing side. He not only attacks the opposing side's position on the issue at hand, he also attacks the opposing team members personally in the most insulting, degrading terms he can imagine.

Bob loves to go after expert witnesses. No matter how much education or experience they have, he makes them look like they are rank amateurs. He attacks their credentials, he challenges their methods, and he disputes their facts. Bob routinely complains that the experts on the opposing team are biased. He claims that they are willing to testify to anything in order to please the clients who are paying the bills. Not surprisingly, Bob "The Tiger" Thompson finds no merit at all in the conclusions of the experts on the opposing team.

"The Tiger" especially loves to go after environmental activists. Before he even gets to the substance of their arguments, he is likely to dismiss them as being "tree-hugging bark eaters who are anti-business, anti-growth, and anti-American." He continues by saying that the environmental activists who are opposing him are completely ignorant. He loves to belittle them. For example, if an environmental group is complaining about the frequency of oil tanker spills on the Texas Gulf Coast, Bob might ridicule the organization by saying, "The members of that environmental organization are so ignorant about the energy industry they couldn't find a can of motor oil in an Exxon service station."

Bob "The Tiger" Thompson, truly an arrogant, obnoxious S.O.B., finds no merit in the arguments of the opposing team. He rejects every point the opposing team makes. Every word that comes from the mouths of his opposition is subject to his ridicule.

He has no interest in compromise, in consensus, or even in simple agreement. His objective is not to beat his opponent. His goal in negotiations is to destroy his opponent.

Bob is not a very nice person to deal with, but many people pay him a great deal of money to be an arrogant, obnoxious S.O.B. People pay him a lot of money because he can be very effective. He can get results for his team. Many opposing team players are intimidated by his arrogance, and they are disgusted with his obnoxious behavior. In many negotiations, however, "The Tiger" gets exactly what he wants.

When should you use the arrogant, obnoxious, S.O.B. approach? First, if you think that the opposing team members are easily intimidated and are lacking in confidence and in self-esteem, the arrogant, obnoxious, S.O.B. approach would probably work. If you believe that the opposing team members are anxious to resolve the negotiation with as little effort and as little conflict as possible, then the S.O.B. approach would probably work for you and for your team. Finally, if the opposing team has one or more arrogant, obnoxious S.O.B. negotiators, you may need to respond in kind in order to protect you and your team members. One way to resist the S.O.B. approach is to get your own S.O.B.s. Have your S.O.B.s tangle with theirs.

Another way to resist the S.O.B. approach is to see it for what it is: a trick designed to cause you to lose your nerve. The lawyer, the S.O.B., is trying to break down your will to fight by attacking you personally. Foil his plans by choosing not to take his attacks personally. Stay relaxed, stay calm, and avoid getting into a fight with him. If he sees that he cannot rattle you, he will leave you alone.

Besides, do you or do any of your teammates want to act like arrogant, obnoxious S.O.B.s? If someone on your team has a decided mean streak, and if that person has the skills to go for the throat, then you might want to use him in this kind of role.

If acting obnoxious and arrogant is not for you or for your team, do not feel obliged to use this technique, even if the opposing team uses it on you. To use this approach properly, you have to be able to separate your public behavior from your private feelings. You have to be willing to forget about tenderness, mercy, fair play, and human kindness.

You also have to be a consummate actor. While you are going after your opponent, you have to convincingly project the belief that you find no redeeming features in him. In the moment that you are attacking your opponent, you have to act as though your opponent has no value in terms of the merits of the issue and no value as a fellow human being.

Most people are not cut out for the arrogant, obnoxious, S.O.B. approach. Most people have too much of the milk of human kindness in them. Besides, there are other approaches that are easier on the psyche that can achieve the same results.

If you find yourself confronted with the arrogant, obnoxious negotiator, and you feel you are not equipped to respond in kind, do not despair. You have two outstanding options available. First, you can keep a tight grip on your self-esteem and you can cheerfully ignore him. Second, you can retain the services of an arrogant, obnoxious S.O.B. for your team. In other words, you can hire a lawyer.

THE "COME LET US REASON TO-GETHER" PREACHER

"Come now, let us reason together."

Book of the Prophet Isaiah, 1:18

When he was confronted with competing and conflicting political advice, President Lyndon Johnson was fond of quoting one phrase from the Book of the Prophet Isaiah: "Come now, let us reason together." Although the quotation was biblical, Johnson's reasons for quoting it were heavily laced with practical political considerations. Lyndon Johnson was, in effect, elevating himself above the fray. He was establishing himself as a higher moral authority who had the power to mediate the controversy. Just as the small town country preacher urges his friends and neighbors to resolve their differences peacefully, Lyndon Johnson was urging the various political interest groups confronting him to reason together in order to resolve their differences.

Johnson was legendary in his ability to mold the thinking of various political groups to suit his point of view. His use of the "come let us reason together" approach was one of the many effective techniques in his massive bag of tricks. The skilled environmental negotiator can also make great progress in advancing his point of view by setting himself up as a "come let us reason together" preacher.

The environmental negotiator who uses this tactic offers his services as a paternal, knowledgeable, impartial mediator for a specific environmental negotiation. Although the environmental negotiator usually has his own set of goals for the negotiation, he professes not to have any personal agenda at all regarding the negotiation if he is using this tactic. He will claim early on in the discussion that he does not have his own point of view regarding the negotiation, that he only wants what is best for all concerned.

His only remarks at the beginning of the debate will be bland, generic, noncontroversial ones. He will urge everyone to get along with one another. He will say, "I only want what is best for our community. Let's try to figure out what we can all agree upon." The "come let us reason together" preacher will stress the importance of a healthy economy and the importance of a healthy environment. He might say, "I want what is best for business and what is best for the environment."

The "come let us reason together" preacher has two purposes in making these noncommittal kinds of statements. First, he is trying to prove to the conflicting parties that he is impartial. Second, he is attempting to establish himself as a higher moral authority on the subject that is being debated.

If the environmental negotiator can convince both sides of the negotiation that he is impartial and that he is operating on a higher moral level than the others in the negotiation, he will be well-positioned to market, very subtly, his own point of view. The "come let us reason together" preacher represents himself as an honest broker, but what he is often doing is quietly pushing his personal point of view.

It is essential that the negotiator who uses this tactic never reveals his personal positions regarding the matter that is being negotiated. If someone asks what his position is, the preacher negotiator should give only the safest, most general responses. If he is asked what he thinks, a good way to handle the question is to reply by stating very specifically what each of the two opposing sides in the negotiation thinks.

Once the preacher negotiator starts giving his point of view, he loses his air of impartiality and his aura of being a higher moral authority. He is reduced to being simply another player on one of the competing teams.

The preacher negotiator influences the debate by getting the two sides to talk to one another face to face. Once the two sides come together and express their respective points of view, the preacher negotiator attempts to shape the negotiation by highlighting the various points on which the two competing teams agree. He attempts to narrow the differences by persuading each side to throw out some items that are offensive to the other side. He tries to retain those items that are pleasing to both sides. The items that are thrown out are usually the items that the preacher negotiator wants thrown out, and the items that are kept are the items that the preacher negotiator wants kept, although he never reveals either of these facts.

If there are sticking points between the two opposing sides, the preacher negotiator orders the two sides to reason together until they resolve their differences. One of the preacher negotiator's techniques for dealing with intransigence is to offer aloud secular "prayers" for peace, for unity, and for harmony. Another technique he uses to resolve irreconcilable differences is to portray in dramatic detail the dire consequences that will result if the two opposing sides fail to reach an agreement. *Endless warfare* and *environmental and financial disaster* are terms that the preacher negotiator frequently uses once he begins to preach to the two opposing teams.

If he is convincing enough, the preacher negotiator can persuade all of the conflicting parties that it is in everyone's best interest to come to an agreement. If the opposing sides continue to resist reaching an agreement, the preacher negotiator's job is to hold the negotiation together until the stubbornness of the two opposing teams begin to crumble.

Politicians love to use the "come let us reason together" preacher tactic because it gives them the opportunity to be a hero to the people on both sides of the negotiation. It is a politician's dream come true to make everybody happy while getting what he wants.

If an environmental negotiator is shrewd, he can use this tactic to get what he wants from a negotiation while appearing to be impartial. He can also have the added benefit of having both sides of the negotiation think that he is a marvelous human being who is operating on a higher moral plane than they are.

This tactic cannot be used at all times in all situations, however. The environmental negotiator may already be a marked individual. His biases and his commitments on given issues may be well known, making it impossible for him to persuade both sides of the negotiation that he is impartial. The environmental negotiator may not have the stature, or the job title, or the finesse required for him to be convincing as a higher moral authority. Finally, the two opposing sides may have differences that are so hostile and so personalized that the environmental negotiator simply cannot persuade them to reason together.

Let me describe for you a time that I used the "come let us reason together" approach during an especially difficult environmental negotiation. The story goes like this.

As part of our city's Master Water Plan, our public works director strongly supported the construction of a concrete dam across the lower reaches of the Trinity River. The main purpose of the dam was not to retain fresh water in a reservoir behind it; its main purpose was to keep saltwater below it from migrating upstream during droughts. Blocking saltwater intrusion would permit the city to take more water from the Trinity River during dry periods.

The environmental community was totally opposed to the concrete dam because it would destroy the most significant estuary on Galveston Bay by sealing off that estuary system. Without the ebb and flow of freshwater and saltwater, the Trinity River estuary would die. The shrimp, the fish, and the other marine life that depended on the estuary would die as well.

As the chairman of the city council committee that was responsible for developing the city Master Water Plan, it was my job to recommend to the full city council whether or not to support the construction of a concrete dam across the lower Trinity River. I decided that, in the face of such profound differences, the best approach would be the "come let us reason together" preacher.

I announced to both sides of the debate that a decision on the lower Trinity River dam had to be made in order to complete the city's Master Water Plan. I said that the best interests of the city would not be served by endless warfare on the issue. I told both sides that each of them had reasonable points of view. The time of stalemate on the issue had to end, I said. It was time for compromise and for agreement.

I asked the public works director and his chief assistants to meet with the leaders of the largest environmental organization in our city. The public works personnel and the environmental leaders agreed to meet with me to conduct negotiations concerning the lower Trinity River dam. I chose the local office of the Sierra Club as the meeting place.

When the two sides gathered together, I proceeded to conduct the meeting. I set the tone by announcing that we were all intelligent, reasonable people who could work out a compromise that was satisfactory to all concerned. I let each side state its goals and its concerns. Then I pointed out, I highlighted, the areas of agreement between the two groups. Both wanted the city to have adequate water supplies in the future; both wanted to protect the marine life in Galveston Bay.

Was there a way, I asked, that we could increase our city's water supplies while preserving the shrimp and the fish in Galveston Bay? After considerable discussion the answer came out. Yes, there was a solution that would permit us to accomplish both goals: build an inflatable barrier that would lie on the river bottom most of the time, but that would inflate to prevent saltwater intrusion during dry periods. This approach would allow the city to maximize its water supply yield from the Trinity River, while protecting the estuary system and the marine life that depended on it.

The "come let us reason together" preacher approach can be resisted if one of the opposing sides, or if both of the opposing sides, make up their minds to be totally unreasonable. Environmental activists are masters at resisting the preacher negotiating tactic. They can be more unreasonable, and unreasonable for longer, than any other players of the game.

In the environmental negotiation described above, both sides chose to be decidedly unreasonable. The dam supporters wanted their concrete dam, and the environmental activists wanted nothing at all constructed on the lower Trinity River. Warfare without ceasing continues, and the inflatable barrier idea remains a flat proposal.

Examine every negotiation to see if the "come let us reason together" approach can be used. Try to imagine in every negotiation whether or not you could play the roles of preacher and of mediator convincingly. It is a difficult act to pull off, but it is an exhilarating feeling to be successful at it.

THE "BORE THEM TO DEATH" APPROACH

> "Every body of law consists essentially in a consistent system of abstract rules which have normally been intentionally established. Furthermore, administration of law is held to consist in the application of these rules to particular cases; the administrative process is the rational pursuit of the interests which are specified in the order governing the corporate group within the limits laid down by legal precepts and following principles which are capable of generalized formulation and are approved in the order governing the group, or at least not disapproved in it."
>
> Max Weber
> *Theory of Social and Economic Organization*

The "bore them to death" approach is the bureaucrat's favorite negotiating style. It is a clever tactic for them to use because it makes them appear to be cooperative while, in reality, they are sucking the life out of their negotiating opposition.

There are a few simple rules for using the "bore them to death" technique. First, never volunteer any useful information to your opposition; make them ask you for it. Second, answer your opponent's questions accurately, but not succinctly. Take your time in responding, and answer at great length. Third, when you answer your opponent's questions, do it in a dull, muffled mono-tone. Remove all emotional content from your voice. Fourth, remove all emotion and all life from the substance of your response. Make certain that your response is not angry, aggressive, cheerful, sad, cute, funny, pleased, or displeased. If you patiently follow these four simple rules, you can bore your opposition to death the way many successful bureaucrats do.

You might ask, "Why would anyone want to bore his opposition to death? Hasn't this book stressed the necessity of getting the opposing team to react?"

True, but sometimes the reaction that you want from the opposing team is for it to go away and leave you and your team alone. It is sometimes difficult to drive the opposition away by using direct forceful action. A far more expedient approach, a far more subtle way to drive your opposition away, is to force them to endure lethal boredom.

I remember well an assistant director of the Public Works Department who was a master at boring his opposition to death. When Russell was questioned by city councilmembers and by the public, he never gave up any information without being forced to do so. If he was asked a direct question, he would respond truthfully and completely. He would respond so truthfully and so completely that his answers could never be measured in tens of seconds. They could only be measured in tens of minutes, that is, tens of minutes for each separate question.

Russell never spoke in short, understandable sentences. His sentences seemed to have no beginning and no ending. They were 50 to 100 words in length. Russell's sentences were longer than most people's paragraphs.

Russell was the original poker face. He never displayed any emotion, no matter how savagely he was attacked. He was like a Bozo the Clown toy. If you knocked him down with an emotional assault, he would immediately right himself and he would regain his emotional equilibrium.

Although Russell always appeared to be politely answering everyone's questions, he answered in such a way that you could never figure out what he was saying. Sometimes he would talk in circles, and sometimes he would go off on tangents.

Russell's voice and word choice were perfect for the "bore them to death" approach. He would drone on and on without ceasing, without changing pitch, without getting louder or softer, without exhibiting any energy or any emotional content. He spoke in departmental jargon, using terms and abbreviations that no one on the opposing team could understand.

He read tables of numbers and cited countless facts in response to each question. If someone asked Russell to explain what those facts and figures meant, he would reply by repeating those facts and figures all over again.

Russell would leave his opponents speechless. His opponents did not understand what he was saying, but they were afraid to ask for clarification. They were afraid to ask Russell for further explanation, but if they did ask them, he would patiently oblige them. He would go back to the beginning, and he would make his whole lifeless, endless, incomprehensible presentation all over again.

After performing this technique for an hour or two, the opposition's will to fight would begin to slip away. Their eyes would glaze over, their spirits would leave their bodies, and the environmental negotiation would quickly be concluded.

The "bore them to death" approach is an excellent tactical choice in two negotiating situations. First, if all you want out of the negotiation is for your opponent to leave you alone, boring them to death is a friendly, effective way to get them to leave you alone. Second, if your primary negotiating goal is inaction, if you want no meaningful action to be taken as a result of the negotiation, the "bore them to death" approach is an outstanding choice.

It is an utterly useless technique if you want any meaningful engagement with the opposing team. It is an excellent tactic for purely defensive purposes. It is a tactic that has no value at all if you want to go on the offensive, or if you want to reach a substantive agreement with your opponents.

The only reliable way to resist the "bore them to death" technique is to avoid negotiating with someone who is skilled at this tactic. There is no foolproof way to beat it. The best you can do is to escape from it as fast as you can.

THE KAMIKAZE PILOT

> "The kamikaze spirit had taken over all of the Japanese armed forces. As Admiral Onishi said, one did not have to have an airplane to have the kamikaze spirit; the principle was to sacrifice one's life in order to strike an effective blow at the enemy."
>
> Edwin P. Hoyt
> *Japan's War*

I believe that everyone is familiar with the Japanese use of kamikaze pilots during the Second World War. As the Allied ships and troops neared the Japanese islands, the Japanese military responded by dispatching many young pilots to their deaths in suicide attacks on Allied shipping. In the ultimate act of self-sacrifice, numerous kamikaze pilots flew their planes into the decks of the approaching ships. Although they were obliterated in the process, the kamikaze pilots caused serious damage to many Allied ships.

It is difficult to understand what would have motivated the kamikaze pilots to destroy themselves in order to inflict maximum damage on the enemy. It is also difficult to imagine how the kamikaze pilot tactic applies to environmental negotiations. Perhaps a definition will help.

The kamikaze pilot technique as I am applying it to environmental negotiations is the art of inflicting maximum public relations damage on the opposing team after it becomes clear that one's negotiating position has become a lost cause. This technique often causes the collateral damage of destroying your team's ability to negotiate with your opponent ever again.

The kamikaze pilot technique is a tactic of last resort, and in many ways it is a tactic that signifies failure. It also can be profoundly self-destructive.

If you and your teammates have tried everything you can think of and it has become clear that you are not going to achieve your negotiating goals, you might want to become the kamikaze pilot. If you have fought the good fight and you are about to go down in flames, the kamikaze tactic is a way that you can salvage a small measure of satisfaction and a portion of your self-respect. I have warned you about the dangers of becoming a kamikaze pilot, but if everything else has failed and you want a pound of flesh from your opposition, here is how you do it.

You use the news media to fry your opposition. You blast the opposing team with one salvo after another. You tell any reporter who will listen every single thing that is wrong with the opposing team and its negotiating position. You admit that your team's position is probably doomed to failure, but you predict in graphic, horrifying detail the terrible consequences that will follow from your opponent's victory.

If you adopt the kamikaze approach, you completely forget about whether or not your statements are offending your opponent. If you are a kamikaze pilot, you do not care whether or not your statements or your actions are personally offensive to the opposing team. Your tactic is not designed to win friends and influence people on the opposing team. The kamikaze tactic is designed to inflict maximum public relations damage on the opposing team.

How long do you carry out the kamikaze pilot technique? As long as a single reporter will listen to you and will report on what you are saying. Once you begin your suicide mission, your only course of action is to shout out your story as long and as loud as you can.

Neither you nor your opponent will have to endure this tactic for a very long time. If you are a successful kamikaze pilot, you will crash your plane, and yourself, into the opposition. Your plane will explode in a great fireball, and the media will dutifully report it. Your opponent will sustain some public relations damage and suffer some ego casualties, and then it will all be over. Your opponent will set about to repair the damage you have done, and you will be dead in terms of future negotiations with the opponent.

There is little that you can do to resist the kamikaze technique if it is used against you. You simply have to absorb the blows for what is usually a brief period of time. If the opposing team begins launching kamikaze attacks against you, do not despair. You should rejoice. It is a sure sign that you have won your environmental negotiation.

Jack Matson, an environmental engineer I know, describes how he used the kamikaze technique in one of his negotiations:

A big multinational firm proposed to locate a copper smelter on the shores of Texas' most prolific estuary — Galveston Bay. Much of the local community welcomed the smelter for the jobs and economic base it would provide. But what a polluter it would be. The permit hearing was clearly wired in favor of the applicant. The opponents — environmental groups, fishermen, and I — blasted the project at every opportunity. We wrote letters to newspapers. We did radio and TV interviews. We talked to every reporter who would listen to us about how bad the copper smelter would be for Galveston Bay. Although the odds were stacked against us, we used kamikaze attacks because we had nothing to lose and a lot to gain if we scored some direct hits.

THE "NOT NEGOTIATING AT ALL" STYLE OF NEGOTIATIONS

"When someone insults you, the most effective response is not to insult him back. The most effective response is to ignore him."

John P. Gorczynski, my dad

One of the shrewdest tactics in environmental negotiations, and one of the most common, is the "not negotiating at all" style of negotiation. This tactic is simple, and it is unnerving to the opposition. Here is how you do it.

Your opposition makes all sorts of attempts to engage you in an environmental negotiation. You and your team ignore those attempts. Your opponent's pleas to negotiate become louder and shriller. You serenely ignore those pleas. Your opponent asks you, point blank, "When are you going to negotiate with us?" You and your team reply, "Negotiate? What negotiations?"

This tactic, if practiced studiously and patiently, can have a devastating effect on the opposing team. It is painful and frightening to be attacked by the opposing team. No one in his right mind likes to be subjected to aggressive insult and public ridicule. The greatest insult you can give any opposing team, however, is not to attack them, but to ignore them. Nothing is more humiliating, nothing is more debilitating.

211

It is a harsh tactic because it projects a profound lack of respect for the views and for the feelings of the fellow human beings on the opposing team. It is a powerfully effective tactic because few individuals and fewer teams have the patience, the coherence, the endurance, and the psychological strength to persist in negotiating after they have been repeatedly ignored.

There are two paradoxes involved in using this style of environmental negotiation. The first paradox is the fact that, although the tactic is based on ignoring the opposition, the one who uses this tactic is very aware of the opposing team and its points of view. Stated another way, ignoring the opposition does not mean being ignorant about them or unaware of their views. The second paradox is the fact that those who use this tactic frequently change their positions to match more closely those of the opposition they are ignoring, even though they never give their opposition credit for causing those changes.

It is because of these two paradoxes that I consider the "not negotiating at all" style to be a true form of negotiation. If one side were totally oblivious to the actions and the intentions of the opposing side, then negotiating would not be taking place. If no movement or adjustments occurred in the positions taken by the side pretending not to negotiate, then the case could be made that no negotiations were happening.

In reality, the side pretending not to negotiate is acutely aware of every word and of every action of the opposing side. The environmental negotiator who pretends not to listen to the views of his opponent listens very intently indeed. When he discovers a need to modify his negotiating positions due to some insight or some pressure provided by the opposition, the "not negotiating at all" negotiator modifies his position.

In reality, the "not negotiating at all" negotiator and his opponents are partners in a most unusual dance. The "not negotiating" negotiator is the silent and invisible dance partner. He makes subtle changes in his movements and in his positions in response to the actions and to the statements of his opponent. In the end, his final negotiating views may even embrace those of his opposition. With a ruthless poetry, however, the "not negotiating at all" negotiator leaves the opposition convinced that it was always dancing alone.

The "not negotiating at all" approach is very familiar to me. I experienced this technique being used by my mayor during my work on water pollution in Lake Houston. Lake Houston provides drinking water for roughly half of Houston. In the early 1980s, sewage contamination from residential developments around the lake threatened this water supply. Several environmental leaders and I campaigned to have the lake cleaned up. The mayor's only response to the media was to say that the lake was perfectly safe.

The media, the public, and concerned environmentalists and scientists tried to confront the mayor with clear evidence of the lake's deterioration. For several weeks, she did not respond.

Out of the blue, the mayor asked me to chair a council committee on Lake Houston. My committee researched the problem of pollution in Lake Houston and described the solution. The solution was simple. The 150 sewer plants in the Lake Houston watershed needed to start properly treating their sewage. Vigorous enforcement in the watershed by city health department personnel would solve the problem.

The mayor and the council adopted my committee's recommendations, and Lake Houston is now clean. But the mayor never acknowledged that the change in her enforcement policy was caused by the media, by concerned scientists and environmentalists, and by me.

PART V:
WINNING AND LOSING

How To Be a Gracious Winner and an Effective Loser — An Introduction

"There's an old saying that victory has 100 fathers and defeat is an orphan."

John F. Kennedy, 1961

"It is not the critic who counts; not the man who points out how the strong man stumbles, or where the doer of deeds could have done them better. The credit belongs to the man who is actually in the arena, whose face is marred with dust and sweat and blood; who strives valiantly; who errs, and comes short again and again, because there is no effort without error and shortcoming; but who does actually strive to do the deeds; who knows the greatest enthusiasms, the greatest devotions; who spends himself in a worthy cause, who at the best knows in the end the triumphs of high achievement, and who at the worst, if he fails, at least fails while daring greatly, so that his place shall never be with those cold and timid souls who know neither victory nor defeat."

Theodore Roosevelt, 1910

You will win some and you will lose some of your environmental negotiations. I will not strain my credibility or explore the limits

217

of your credulity by telling you, "It matters not whether you've won or lost, but how you've played the game."

It matters plenty whether you've won or lost. I've won and I've lost environmental negotiations. Believe me, winning is better.

Winning is better, but it does matter how you play the game of environmental negotiation. To be a great environmental negotiator, you have to be able to win or to lose with class and with style. You have to be able to win graciously and to lose effectively. You have to master the arts of winning and of losing, not just because it is good for you personally, but because it is good for you as an environmental negotiator.

The ending of one environmental negotiation is usually the beginning of another. The way you win and the way you lose your current environmental negotiation will play a big role in determining your success or your failure in future negotiations.

A Word About Winning and Losing

Some people are uncomfortable applying the terms *winning* and *losing* to environmental negotiations. I am not. I have never seen an environmental negotiation in which there were neither winners nor losers. Usually there are winners on one side and there are losers on the other. Occasionally both sides are winners, and sometimes, both sides are losers. But always there are winners or there are losers.

What determines if you should consider yourself a winner or a loser in a particular environmental negotiation? I have a very practical method for determining whether or not I have won an environmental negotiation. I ask myself one question. Did I achieve enough of my goals to be satisfied with the results of the environmental negotiation? If the answer to this question is yes, then I consider myself a winner. If the answer to this question is no, then I consider myself a loser concerning this particular negotiation.

Do I worry about whether or not the players on the opposing side achieved their goals? Usually, I do not. It is not my purpose in life and it is not my mission as an environmental negotiator to make certain that the opposing side wins. I am interested in seeing that my side wins. I am not overly concerned with whether or not the other team wins. If I achieve my goals in a negotiation, I am happy. It is the responsibility of the players on the opposing team to worry about achieving their goals.

You should pursue achieving your goals for an environmental negotiation with an attitude of civilized ruthlessness. Stay within the law, abide by the rules of the game, and show a reasonable amount of courtesy to your opponent. But remember that environmental negotiations are not an exercise in human sensitivity training. You should never say to your opponent, "Your goals are OK, and my goals are OK," unless you really mean it or unless it is a ruse to relax your opponent before you pounce on him.

If your goals are truly compatible with the goals of your opponent, then the possibility exists that both of you could conclude your environmental negotiation as winners. If common goals exist, you should rejoice. You should highlight those common goals. You can exploit those shared goals to achieve many other goals that you do not share with your opponent.

If common, compatible goals do not exist between you and your opponent, then you should concentrate on winning the negotiation and on beating your opponent. You should not spend any time during the negotiation worrying about how your opponent will feel if he loses.

During the heat of an environmental negotiation, you must conquer your own fears of losing. While you are engaged in a negotiation, do not dwell on how you will feel if you lose. When the negotiation is over and you have lost the negotiation, then you can worry about your feelings regarding losing.

The best time to deal with your feelings about the outcome of a particular negotiation is after that negotiation is concluded. That is also the best time to deal with your opponent's feelings about the results of the negotiation.

In the next several pages, I will discuss the four possible outcomes of environmental negotiations. I will suggest methods for handling your feelings about winning and about losing. I will also suggest ways of dealing with your opponent's responses to winning and to losing.

The Four Possible Outcomes of an Environmental Negotiation

There are four possible conclusions to an environmental negotiation. They are as follows:

1. Your team wins, their team loses.
2. Your team wins, their team wins.
3. Your team loses, their team wins.
4. Your team loses, their team loses.

You will vary your behavior according to the circumstances and according to the results of your particular negotiation.

Now I know someone out there is saying, "What about a stalemate? What about the times when a negotiation ends with no movement at all on either side?" My response is, if no movement was the primary goal of both sides, then both teams are winners. If some movement was the goal of both sides, then both of them are losers. Finally, if one side wanted movement and the other side did not, then the side that wanted movement is the loser, and the side that wanted no movement is the winner. I believe that even a negotiation that ends in a stalemate has winners and losers.

OUTCOME NUMBER ONE — YOUR TEAM WINS AND THEIR TEAM LOSES

If your team wins and their team loses, the most important thing for you to do is to let the opposing team down as gently as you can. It is rarely to your benefit to gloat over your victory.

There are no advantages in humiliating and in angering your opponent after you have defeated him. Rubbing your win in your opponent's face will make him angrier than he already is; and remember, anger is a potent form of human energy that can be used against you. Once you have achieved your goals and the negotiation is concluded, you and your team should do everything in your power to lessen the anger and the embarrassment of the opposing team.

There are several ways to let the opposing team down gently when you win and they lose. One of the simplest ways to accomplish this is to compliment the opposing team's players on their performance. Flattery only works if you are sincere, so make certain that your compliments have a legitimate basis in fact.

Recall those parts of the opposing team's work that impressed you and compliment them, publicly and privately, on those aspects of the negotiation. If they were eloquent speakers, tell them and tell the press how impressed you were with their speeches. If they demonstrated bulldog tenacity during the negotiation, tell them and tell the news media how much you respect their persistence and their determination. A few sincere, well-chosen compliments will begin to diffuse the opposing team's anger over your victory and its defeat.

A second approach to use when you win and they lose is to try to persuade the opposing team that they did not really lose. It is a neat trick if you can pull it off, but it is certainly a delicate operation to perform. This tactic will greatly ease the anger of the opposing players, if you are successful at it. It will infuriate them even further if you attempt this approach and you fail.

You persuade the opposing team members that they did not really lose by claiming that you modified your negotiating goals considerably after you heard their arguments. You give them credit for many of the results of the negotiation, and you try to convince them that some of the results that occurred were outcomes that they wanted.

It will be difficult to convince them that they are not losers if they do not see any of their negotiating goals in the conclusion of the negotiation. You will have to persuade them that achieving your goals in reality helps them realize their goals. If there is little truth in it, it can be a tough sell. I wish you luck.

A third way to handle your winning and their losing is to distract them from their current defeat by recalling past negotiations that they won or by predicting future negotiations in which they will be victorious. Citing previous successes of your opponent is usually a great deal more persuasive technique than predicting future successes, but you do the best you can with what you've got. If you have no negotiating history with your opponent, or if you have beaten him in all previous negotiations, then the best you can do is to say, "You will probably beat us next time."

Outcome Number Two — Your Team Wins and Their Team Wins

An environmental negotiation in which both teams truly win is an uncommon event. I am not saying that it never happens because, from time to time, it does occur. Both teams winning is an unusual natural phenomena, like, say, a lunar eclipse. You will probably experience it a couple of times during your career as an environmental negotiator, but the planets have to be aligned just right, and you have to be observant to notice the phenomenon when it comes along.

It is not difficult to know how to behave properly when both teams win. The proper thing to do when both teams accomplish their negotiating goals is to publicly celebrate the event. Your team and the opposing team need to stage an orgy of public self-congratulations.

At the very least, have a joint press conference in which you and your opponent take turns praising each other and giving each other all of the credit for the success of the negotiation. Take praise and lay it on thick. Gush shamelessly about how wonderful your opponent is.

Joint press conferences are fine, but they can be a little tame.

223

More in keeping with the extraordinary nature of your negotiation is to have a full-blown party. If your team and the opposing team have successfully negotiated the construction of a new sewer treatment plant, a goal that both of you shared, then have a sewer plant opening day party. Cut the ceremonial ribbon. Have the leaders of the two opposing teams turn on the pumps to start plant operations. Bring in a loud and decidedly upbeat band to play for the occasion. Pass out commemorative buttons. Serve free food and drinks, and definitely invite the news media to come out and to act silly with you.

Whether you decide on the more sedate joint press conference or you opt for the more appropriate kind of celebration, be sure to highlight and to celebrate the fact that both sides won. Point out this fact to the public at large through the news media and privately be sure to say it to your opponent. Nothing poisons a joint victory faster than for one side to act as though it was the only side that won.

Finally, remember to share the credit with your opponent for the success of the negotiation. Your opponent's affection for you will quickly sour if he sees that you are trying to hog all of the glory for the negotiating miracle that both of you share.

Outcome Number Three — Your Team Loses and Their Team Wins

I hate to lose an environmental negotiation. I particularly hate to lose when the opposing team wins. My first instinct is to fly a kamikaze plane right into the largest aircraft carrier on the opposing side.

As I explained earlier in this book, that response is inherently self-destructive. Sometimes it is the only way to preserve your sense of dignity, but more often it is a suicidal act of frustration that yields nothing positive for you.

There are two other responses that are available to you that are far more constructive. Those two choices are

1. You can decide to change your negotiating goals after the negotiation is completed and declare victory. You can say that the goals that your opponent achieved were the goals you, too, wanted to achieve all along.
2. You can admit to your opponent and to the world that you lost the negotiation. In other words, you can accept your loss and be big about it.

I am not crazy about either one of these two choices. I find it profoundly phoney to change my negotiating goals at the end of the negotiation in order to be able to declare victory. If there is a shred of the truth in it, I can sometimes be coaxed to do it.

I am normally too proud to lie about my true negotiating intentions once the negotiation has concluded. I have seen several environmental negotiators, however, who have an unbelievable ability to adjust their goals to fit the outcome of the negotiation.

I have known several politicians and a handful of bureaucrats who never lose an environmental negotiation. Whatever the results of the negotiation, those are the results that these politicians and these bureaucrats wanted. They never lose, or at least, they never admit to losing.

I am more comfortable with the second approach. I would rather admit my loss, be big about it, and go on to the next negotiation. I am convinced that this kind of honesty lays the groundwork for future successful negotiations with your victorious opponent. There is no guarantee that your opponent will negotiate with you in the future, but he is more likely to do so if you show some class by acknowledging your defeat.

You don't have to grovel or to get down on your knees. It is more appropriate to be quietly defiant, bloodied but unbowed, in announcing your loss. You can say that you and your team will be back to fight another day and that next time you expect to prevail. But admit to your opponent that he has beaten you this time. He will respect you for doing it, and he will probably give you the opportunity to beat him on another day in another negotiation.

OUTCOME NUMBER FOUR — YOUR TEAM LOSES AND THEIR TEAM LOSES

The saddest of all environmental negotiations are the ones in which nobody wins, that is, negotiations in which neither side gets what it wants. An environmental negotiation in which both sides lose is failure raised by the power of 2. It is failure squared.

Your greatest temptation after experiencing this type of negotiation is to quit the game altogether. There is an overpowering desire to give up environmental negotiations entirely after a lose-lose.

If you lose and your opponent loses, both of you are filled with guilt, frustration, anger, and depression. Take my word for it, it is harder to accept a negotiating conclusion in which nobody wins than it is to accept a negotiating conclusion in which your side loses and the other side wins.

Under the second circumstance, at least somebody is happy. With the losing-all-around result, nobody is happy.

There is an enormous temptation to blame the opposing team for the dismal result. "If they were not so stupid or so unreasonable or so inflexible," you say to yourself, "this negotiation could have been concluded successfully." After a lose-lose negotiation, you will find yourself mentally accusing the opposing team and cursing them under your breath.

It is perfectly all right to say rude things about your opponent, and it is perfectly acceptable to curse your opponent, as long as you keep it to yourself. No useful purpose is served in verbally flogging your opponent and in publicly blaming him for your shared failure.

It is extremely difficult, and very expensive in terms of time and energy, to try to breathe life back into a failed negotiation. If the conditions were not conducive to someone's success the first time around, they are not likely to be conducive to anybody's success the second time around.

If you and your opponent have a failed negotiation, you do not need more negotiations. You need group therapy or environmental marriage counseling. You need a wise environmental negotiator that both sides trust to enter the picture. The environmental counselor can sit down with the two sides, and he can attempt to reconcile their irreconcilable differences. He can use the "come let us reason together" approach to salvage the negotiation. This type of therapy is one healthy response to a negotiation in which both sides lose.

Another healthy response is to "shake the dust off of your sandals and to move on." Acknowledge that the outcome was unsatisfactory to both sides, but be gentle about it. Be gentle to yourself, and be gentle to your opponent. Accept both of your limitations, forget about blame, and prepare to move on to another negotiation.

The world of environmental negotiation is a big place. There is no benefit in continuing a negotiation in which everybody loses.

PART VI:

CONCLUSION

CONCLUSION

"No plan survives an encounter with the enemy."

A time-honored military strategist's maxim

"In any battle, there is always the fog of combat."

Hear in countless T.V. interviews
during the U.S. and Coalition Forces war with Iraq

I shared a lot with you in this book. You now understand the unique characteristics of environmental negotiations, and you are familiar with the various kinds of environmental negotiations: formal and informal, public and private. You can see how the roles of the media change to fit the various kinds of environmental negotiations.

I gave you a program that lists the players of the game. You recognize and can call by name engineers and politicians, bureaucrats and environmental activists, industrialists and developers. You better understand the people and the media. You have become wise in the ways of lawyers, lobbyists, and other hired guns, and you are constantly searching for translators, primary leaders, and bridgebuilders.

I told you the story of Sam Houston and the Alamo. You will always follow the five strategic steps that Sam Houston did: do research, take stock, organize, act, and react.

I introduced you to some fine tactics. Etched in your mind forever are the blacksmith and the surgeon, the "know-it-all" expert and the warm, friendly negotiator. You will always remember the arrogant, obnoxious S.O.B, the "come let us reason together" preacher, and the "bore them to death" bureaucrat. You will never forget the kamikaze pilot or the negotiator who pretends not to be negotiating at all.

Finally, I taught you about winning and losing. You now know how to win with style and how to lose with dignity. You are going to be a gracious winner and an effective loser.

I have told you everything. Well, almost everything. I suppose we have reached the point in your training where I must give you some final, fatherly advice. With considerable embarrassment and discomfort, I have to share with you the environmental negotiating facts of life.

The first fact of life is that real environmental negotiations are never as clear and neat and orderly as I have portrayed them in the book. You are not always going to be able to perform the five strategic steps in a leisurely, measured manner. Sometimes you are going to have to perform all five steps simultaneously. Sometimes the order of the steps gets all messed up in the heat of the moment. Opponents don't always cooperate by behaving in predictable ways. The various players of the game act strangely and unpredictably abandon their stereotypes.

The second fact of life is that you are on your own out there. Even though I have given you a boatload of terrific tactics to use, you are the one who is going to have to decide when and how and whether to use them. It is your team that is on the field. You are the coach. You have to call the plays. It is difficult to make good decisions while the big game is being played. The fog of combat is always present in environmental negotiations.

The third fact of life is that you may find that none of the tactics I have given you apply to your specific environmental negotiation. You may discover, to your horror, that no known tactic exists to deal with your particular negotiating situation. Rather than give up the fight, I urge you and your teammates to dream up some new tactics. Probe the limits of your creativity. Try a worthwhile, untested approach. If it works, you may someday have the satisfaction of telling me, yourself, and your teammates that you are much smarter than I am.

The fourth and final fact of life is that environmental negotiations are not a game. I know, I know. I have spent the entire book convincing you that they are a game, and now, at the end, I pull the rug out from under you.

Sorry, there is no Santa Claus, and environmental negotiations are not a game. No human activity is more important than environmental negotiation and no human responsibility is more solemn than being an environmental negotiator. I conclude with a quote from John F. Kennedy:

> "Never before has man had such capacity to control his own environment, to end thirst and hunger, to conquer poverty and disease, to banish illiteracy and massive human misery. We have the power to make this the best generation of mankind in the history of the world — or to make it the last."

REFERENCES

I used the following references in the preparation of my book:

Alinsky, S.D., *Rules for Radicals* (New York: Random House, 1971).

Bartlett, J., *Familiar Quotations* (Boston: Little Brown, 1980).

Blau, P.M., *Bureaucracy in Modern Society* (New York: Random House, 1956).

Carroll, L., *Alice's Adventures in Wonderland* (London: Oxford University Press, 1971).

Cooley, Denton A., *Reflections and Observations: Essays of Denton A. Cooley* (Austin, TX: Eakin Press, Inc., 1984).

Fehrenbach, T.R., *Lone Star, A History of Texas and the Texans* (New York: Collier Books, 1985).

Grove, P.B., *Webster's Third New International Dictionary of the English Language* (Springfield, MA: G.&C. Merriam Co., 1963).

Hoyt, E.P., *Japan's War* (New York: McGraw Hill, 1986).

Matson, J.V., *Effective Expert Witnessing* (Chelsea, MI: Lewis Publishers, Inc., 1990).

Oxford Annotated Bible (New York: Oxford University Press, 1965).

Oxford Dictionary of Quotations (New York: Oxford University Press, 1979).

Platt, S., Ed., *Respectfully Quoted* (Washington, D.C.: Library of Congress, 1989).

Tzu, S., *The Art of War* (New York: Oxford University Press, 1963).

Weber, M., *Theory of Social and Economic Organization* (New York: Oxford University Press, 1947).

Zartman, W.I., and Berman, M., *The Practical Negotiator* (New Haven, CT: Yale University Press, 1981).

INDEX

237